LIFE IN THE GOOD SHEPHERD'S FLOCK

Meditations on Psalm 23

Michael L. Faber

Elk Grove Publications
Elk Grove, CA

ISBN-13: 978-1-94078-23-5

Copyright ©2019 Michael L. Faber

All rights reserved. No part of this publication may be reproduced or distributed in any form or by any means, electronic or mechanical, without prior permission in writing from the publisher.

Requests for permission to make copies of any part of this work should be emailed to mfaber@elkgrove.net, subject line "permissions." Publisher hereby grants permission to reviewers to quote up to 100 words from up to three chapters in their reviews, and requests that hyperlinks to said reviews be emailed to the address above or physical copies mailed to the address below.

Elk Grove Publications
9124 Ek Grove Blvd.
Elk Grove, CA 95624
Untied States of America

Cover photoS ©2019 Michael L. Faber. All rights reserved.

Printed in United States of America

CONTENTS

THE LORD IS MY SHEPHERD: INTRODUCTION . . 1
1. A GOD WHO PROVIDES 7
2. A GOD WHO GUIDES 24
3. A GOD WHO GIVES BACK 42
4. A GOD WITH A REPUTATION TO KEEP 53
5. A GOD WITH US 64
6. A GOD WHO CELEBRATES 79
7. A GOD WHO ANOINTS 90
8. A GOD WHOSE MERCY IS BEFORE & AFTER . 100
9. A GOD OF ETERNAL ABIDING 110
ABOUT THE AUTHOR 117
ACKNOWLEDGMENTS 118

THE LORD IS MY SHEPHERD

INTRODUCTION

The 23rd Psalm is one of the most beloved chapters in the Bible. In that famous passage, David pens these words, "The LORD is my shepherd". Throughout this book, we will flesh out each line of the 23rd Psalm and look at how David describes how God serves as his Shepherd. Before we jump in, however, I would like to take a quick look at the biblical concept of shepherd.

If a modern writer were writing a praise to the LORD, he probably would choose a different metaphor. He might write the LORD is my Guide, Father, Team Leader, Drill Sergeant, or Lover or any other word that pertains more to modern life. We would probably not choose the word shepherd, unless we were thinking of biblical examples, because we don't really think about shepherds, or often see them in our modern lives. When is the last time you actually saw a shepherd that wasn't in a Bible movie? Thinking of the LORD as his shepherd was entirely natural for David, because He was a shepherd before he became a warrior and a king. He may have even composed this psalm during the time that he served as a shepherd for his father Jesse's flocks. We can easily imagine him sitting out on a lonely field staring out at his flock of sheep and thinking about all the duties he had towards these sheep. Eventually, the thought may have occurred to him, "Hey, God does all the same things for me that I do for my sheep!"

The idea of shepherd is deeply ingrained in Jewish biblical history. After all, Abraham, Isaac and Jacob were shepherds. When Joseph brought his family to Egypt, he had to tell Pharaoh that his family were shepherds and tended livestock, even though "all shepherds are detestable to the Egyptians" (Gen. 46:34).

Certainly, the Jews did other jobs once they settled in Egypt. Eventually, they were turned into slaves that made bricks. When they obtained their freedom and settled in the promised land, they took many positions and many career paths. As pointed out, however, their beloved King David began his career as a shepherd and penned the beloved words of the 23rd Psalm identifying the LORD as his Shepherd. This identification of the LORD with the concept of shepherd continued later by the Jewish Prophets.

The LORD told Isaiah to speak these words of comfort to His people, "He tends his flock like a shepherd; He gathers the lambs in his arms and carries them close to his heart; he gently leads those that have young" (Isa 40:11 NIV). In these words, the LORD contrasts his impending judgment with the imagery of Himself as a loving and caring shepherd gently taking care of his lambs and treating them with love and compassion.

Michael L. Faber

In speaking his prophecies of impending judgment on Jerusalem, Jeremiah comforts his people with the notion that once the judgment is over, "He who scattered Israel will gather them and will watch over his flock like a shepherd" (Jer 31:10 NIV). Jeremiah invokes the image of God as shepherd who will find the sheep scattered by trouble and hardship, bring them together, watch over them, and protect them.

In the Bible, the term shepherd did not always refer to God. The term was used to refer to religious or political leaders of the day. These uses were rarely good. God gave Jeremiah words of prophecy against the leaders of Judah. "'Woe to the shepherds who are destroying and scattering the sheep of my pasture!' declares the LORD. Therefore, this is what the LORD, the God of Israel, says to the shepherds who tend my people: 'Because you have scattered my flock and driven them away and have not bestowed care on them, I will bestow punishment on you for the evil you have done,' declares the LORD" (Jer. 23:1-2 NIV). In light of the behavior of these bad shepherds, God promised, "'I myself will gather the remnant of my flock out of all the countries where I have driven them and will bring them back to their pasture where they will be fruitful and increase in number. I will place shepherds over them who will tend them, and they will no longer be afraid or terrified, nor will any be missing', declares the LORD" (Jer 23:3-4 NIV). God was about to address the behavior of the bad shepherds, fix the problem, and put good shepherds, (eg. good kings, and religious leaders) over the land.

During the time of exile, God reminded Ezekiel that due to the failures of the human shepherds, the LORD, Himself would be the Shepherd of Israel. "'For this is what the

Sovereign LORD says: 'I myself will search for my sheep and look after them. As a shepherd looks after his scattered flock when he is with them, so will I look after my sheep. I will rescue them from all the places where they were scattered on a day of clouds and darkness. I will bring them out from the nations and gather them from the countries, and I will bring them into their own land. I will pasture them on the mountains of Israel, in the ravines and in all the settlements of the land'" (Ezek. 34:11-13 NIV). In the following words, he promises to "tend them in a good pasture" where they will "lie down" (Ezek 34:14-15 NIV) "search for the lost…bind up the injured and strengthen the weak" (Ezek. 34:16 NIV). He also promises to judge his flock and separate the fat sheep from the lean sheep, and to place over them "one shepherd, my servant David" (Ezek 34:21-22 NIV). This leads us to the point where God promises to shepherd His flock directly, while at the same time appointing his "servant David" to shepherd them. How can He do this? We know now that He fulfilled both of these promises concurrently by appointing His only Begotten Son, Jesus, who is also the Son of David, to shepherd His people.

We are all familiar with Jesus' proclamation, "I am the good shepherd. The good shepherd lays down his life for the sheep" (John 10:11 NIV). Jesus contrasts Himself as the good shepherd with the hired hand. The Good Shepherd is willing to pay any price to protect his sheep, even his own life, while the hired hand runs away at the first sign of danger. This is reminiscent of the words of Ezekiel when he described the bad shepherds who allowed the sheep to be scattered. The LORD promised through Ezekiel that He Himself would shepherd His people, and now Jesus Christ, who is God in the flesh, has announced the fulfillment of that promise. Indeed, He is the

Good Shepherd. What does the good shepherd do? He lays his life down for the sheep, if necessary, to keep them safe. Jesus Christ did exactly this when He laid His life down on the cross in order to die for your sins and mine. We are His sheep, and He laid His life down for our protection.

In Jesus, we see the New Testament idea of the LORD as Shepherd. Now that we have reviewed what the entire Bible has to say about this subject, let us return to the beautiful words of David in Psalm 23.

1.

A GOD WHO PROVIDES

"The LORD is my shepherd; I shall not want"(Psalm 23:1 KJV).

How many of you have ever been unemployed? How many of you have ever been hungry and not known where your next meal will come from? How many of you have lost a spouse? How many have been alienated from beloved family members? How many have suffered debilitating sickness?

Almost all of us have suffered great loss, or will someday. The truth is, loss is part of our experience of living, whether or not we are people of faith.

As I read this Scripture, "The LORD is my shepherd, I shall not want," I thought, "This simply isn't true. We all want. We all lack at some time in our life." My friends, let me tell you a rule I have when interpreting Scripture. It is a simple rule which has three parts: **1) God's word is always true: 2) If the way I am reading God's word leads me to suspect that**

God's word is not true, then 3) I know I am not reading and interpreting God's word correctly.

Therefore, since I know, from time to time, we all suffer shortage and loss and desire things that we never attain, then I must avoid reading the Scripture to mean that I will never want anything when the LORD is my Shepherd. So how should I read it? What does this passage really mean?

When we wonder what the Bible actually means, it is best to look at the original language, because sometimes translations can be deceiving. Psalm 23 was written in Hebrew. Words may have several meanings in their translated language, but the original language helps us narrow down which of these meanings is correct. For instance, the word "want" has several meanings in English. The most common modern meaning of want (which is not the Hebrew meaning), is to desire something. For instance, I want a hamburger. I want a new car. Is God promising to fulfill our every whim and desire? Some "name it and claim it" preachers might want you to think so. But what does the Hebrew *really* mean?

By looking at the original Hebrew, we see the word *kheser* means to lack.

The LORD is my Shepherd, I will not lack. We can understand the passage to mean that when the LORD is our Shepherd we will not lack (any necessity). Is this speaking of food and material things alone, or something more? We can gain hints by looking how a particular word is used elsewhere in the Scripture.

According to Strong's concordance, this Hebrew word *kheser* appears only one other time in the Bible.

Michael L. Faber

"The righteous eateth to the satisfying of his soul; but the belly of the wicked shall want" (Proverbs 13:25 KJV). This is the literal translation of the Hebrew. Notice how righteous is contrasted to wicked, satisfaction is contrasted with want (*kheser*), and soul is contrasted with belly. While belly might infer eating or food, the word *beten* is also used to denote a seat of hunger, passion, avarice, and the inmost part of man. Thus in the KJV, we see that the soul of the righteous is satisfied, but the inner parts of the wicked feel a lacking akin to hunger. We are getting closer to the original intention. I will point out a major problem here. The NIV comes up with a more material translation of this proverb, "The righteous eat to their heart's content, but the stomach of the wicked goes hungry" (Prov 13:25 NIV). NIV does a dynamic, (rather than literal) translation trying to guess the authors intent and put it into modern language. The problem is that this statement just isn't true. In our experience, are the wicked really the ones who go hungry, or is it the righteous? Are the wicked the poor and the righteous rich? No. It is usually the opposite. One need look no further than other psalms, such as Psalm 73 in which the psalmist complains, "For I envied the arrogant when I saw the prosperity of the wicked. They have no struggles; their bodies are healthy and strong" (Ps 73:3-4).This comes closer to the realities of real life than the idea that the wicked go without enough to eat and sufficient material possessions. Using my rule of interpretation that Scripture is always true, and if we read it in a certain way that it seems to be false, we must be reading it wrong, we can conclude that the NIV dynamic translation is wrong. But, the KJV (and the original Hebrew) give us a way of reading these two Scriptures in a way that is true. When we trust in the LORD, we are satisfied (at least spiritually, but often physically as well). When we don't trust in the LORD, and we follow the ways of the wicked, we lack something inside and can feel it like a hunger.

This way of looking at things makes more sense. One reason the wicked are often wealther than the righteous is that the wicked seem to have an insatiable desire to accumulate wealth, even if it means cutting corners, breaking laws, hurting people, or any other behavior that gets them what they think they want. Yet, no matter how much they get, they always want more. Their stomach, or their inner being, feels hunger or lack, which they cannot fill, no matter how many possessions they accumulate. The righteous, on the other hand, are not willing to break the rules, avoid paying taxes, or hurt people, and therefore they accumulate less. They do not have an insatiable hunger driving them to get more and more, because they are satisfied. They realize that many things in life are more important than money. They eat to the satisfying of their soul, but no more.

A key concept to understand is that the righteous are satisfied with less, while the unrighteous are dissatisfied no matter how much they have.

LORD OF THE HARVEST

In line with the LORD being our Shepherd who ensures that we do not lack what we need, we also know Him as the "LORD of the Harvest." Jesus referred to Him as such when He stated "Ask the LORD of the harvest, therefore, to send out workers into His harvest field" (Matt 9:38 NIV). Jesus called the Father, the LORD of the Harvest. In Matthew 9, Jesus taught that God would bring in the harvest of souls, but

He was also speaking of a great Old Testament truth. Part of the Old Testament covenant was to thank God for the harvest in a series of festivals, the Feast of the Tabernacles, the Feast of Unleavened Bread and the Feast of Weeks. The reason for celebrating was because "the LORD your God will bless you in all your harvest and in all the work of your hands, and your joy will be complete" (Deut 16:15 NIV).

If any of you have ever been farmers, you will realize that your livelihood is beyond your control. You can plant all the right seeds and use all the right fertilizer, but if the weather is too hot or too cold, you will lose your crop. If there is too little or too much rain, you will lose your crop. If a swarm of insects or birds comes down on your land, you will lose your crop. Economic conditions can also make or break you. Life is out of your control. Understanding this, it is easy to become a praying man or woman. Farmers realize that their future rests in the LORD's hands and not theirs. Of course, the same is true for the rest of us in non-agricultural jobs. Our futures and economic prosperity, while somewhat determined by our hard work and skill, often rest on factors beyond our control.

Looking quickly at Deuteronomy 16:15, God instructed the Israelites to conduct three agricultural festivals a year to thank Him and in exchange God would 1) bless their Harvest, 2) bless the work of their hands, and 3) make their joy complete. We understand how the LORD of the Harvest can ensure that their harvest will be plentiful. He can fix the weather, control the bugs, etc.

He also promises to bless the work of their hands. I have a question for you. Have you ever tried to do something but found that nothing is going right? The harder you try, the more it goes wrong? Perhaps you get to the point where you forget the scriptural admonition, "Do not let any unwholesome talk come out of your mouths" (Eph. 4:29 NIV)? I have. Then at that moment of despair and defeat, have you ever remembered that perhaps, just maybe, you should pray about it to the LORD, and after doing so, everything seems to fall into place? I have. Praise the LORD! How much frustration, anger, and worry could have been avoided if I had just prayed at first? But thankfully, the LORD came through once I did pray. This is an example of blessing the work of your hands. When we come to the LORD in thanksgiving and prayer, He blesses our harvest, and He blesses the work of our hands. Finally, He makes our joy complete. We will talk about this later in the chapter.

God often operates in this manner, because He wants us to come to Him frequently. He could just bless us once by giving us a magic ring so that everything we touch prospers, but experience proves that we would quickly forget about Him and His desire for our lives. How many Hollywood and Rock n Roll stars have died from suicide or drug abuse? We are not designed for constant prosperity and ease.

God's plan for us (His sheep) requires that we learn to depend on Him. In the Lord's Prayer, Jesus reminds us to pray for our daily bread. He didn't say that we should pray, "Give us today all the bread we will ever need to retire comfortably" but rather, "Give us this day, our **daily** bread." This reminds us of the time that He led Israel through the desert and provided them with mana to survive, but specifically told them to gather no more than they needed for the day, except on Fridays when they could gather two day's supply so they could rest on Saturday (their Sabbath). Those that tried to gather more than they needed quickly found they had a pot of maggots! God fed the people of Israel in the desert as much as they needed to survive, but not necessarily what they wanted.

This leads us to our next spiritual principle when meditating on the passage, "The LORD is my shepherd, I shall not want." This principle is as follows: **As people of God, even though we will not want, we also might not get what we want.** The corollary to this principle is that **God doesn't need to give us lots of material goodies to lead us into a satisfying and joyful life.**

I learned this lesson in 1993, when I took my first trip to Vietnam. When I visited my family and the surrounding neighborhoods, I realized that they didn't have much. Few had TV's. Few had refrigerators. No one had a computer. No one had a telephone. Houses were made of concrete block with cement floors. Carpets were optional. They did not have modern bathrooms or showers or comfortable furniture to sit on. No one had a car. They got around on mopeds and bicycles. Despite all of this material poverty, they had neighbors and family who visited, and the local church which they all attended. In spite of the absence of comfort and technology, they seemed to lead happier and more joyful lives than the people I knew in the United States. What brought them happiness was not things but faith, family, and friends. Certainly, there is nothing wrong with possessing things which provide you convenience and comfort. Just don't let those things possess you. Sometimes God allows us to learn this lesson the hard way.

I have been reading a book called, "God's Provision in Tough Times: True Stories of People who have Experienced Miracles in Tough Times," by Cynthia Howerter and La-Tan Roland Murphy. I came to the book with different expectations for the stories than was actually delivered. I was expecting a series of 'in the nick of time' miracles, where just the right amount of money was given at just the right time. There were a few of those, but mostly, the 25 true stories were about people facing tough times through illness or unemployment. These people had to cut back. They had to let go of treasured possessions, houses, cars, jobs, and status. While the paring back was painful and difficult, they learned that God still came through for them when it really mattered. Their needs were met, but not all of their wants. What they gained in those periods of hardship was a greater reliance on God, and on each other.

One of my favorite stories in the book was about a family who experienced a financial set back which led to loss of their family home. They had a number of fig trees on their property. They used the fruit from these trees to make cakes and cookies and give them to the poor. This ministry gave them great personal fulfillment and was their special gift to God. As they lost their home, part of the loss was the realization that they would never be able to perform this ministry again. In spite of their lower income, God opened the heart of a landlord who had an old, run-down house for rent. The LORD caused the landlord to rent to the family for less than the market rental value. This discount was a gift from God and made it possible for the family to at least live in a detached single family dwelling instead of having to rent a room. While they were grateful to God for his provision of a home, even if it was run-down, as they moved their things, they felt loss in their hearts. Loss of the newer house for the old broken-down one. Loss of their ministry. Suddenly, as they were moving their possessions they noticed that among the trees in the backyard was a fig tree! What were the chances that this old house would contain a fig tree? Now they could retain part of their identity. Now they could continue their fig tree ministry. Now they knew that God still had their back!

A great truth of the Christian faith is that we have a God in heaven who is able to supply all of our needs and who desires that we come to Him with our needs on a daily basis. We will explore this more in the next chapter.

While we cannot declare that God always provides food when we are hungry or drink when we are thirsty (because many people of faith have died in famines and droughts), we can claim as an element of our faith, that absent some other overriding plan, God delights in coming through for us in our moment of need and that provision of material necessities is certainly part of the provision our LORD brings us and certainly part of His not allowing us to want.

HE PROVIDES MORE THAN FOOD OR WATER

Of course, our LORD provides for our needs in many different ways and different circumstances.

About 15 years ago, I received a vision from the LORD to construct an after-school facility for South East Asian kids in a gang infested neighborhood of South Sacramento, California. I felt this was a real vision from God and gathered a number of people to support it. I looked around the neighborhood for the perfect location and saw an old, abandoned, broken-down medical building. I approached the landlord, Dr. Hung Gia Hoang, with my vision and it turned out that he not only was a Christian but told me he would give our group the building for free if we would complete the construction! Praise the LORD! He had provided us with a place, but we still lacked funds for construction. We also needed permission from the city to establish a community center, for which we needed certified architectural plans. We found an architect, but he would not do the work for free. He wanted $5,000.00. We did not have this money. We prayed and fasted, and within days, we received word that a woman unknown to us had donated $5,000.00! We praised God as He continued to provide confirmation that this plan was truly from Him. We lacked building funds, but it turned out that the landlord had some insurance claims for prior vandalism on that building and he let us submit the claims and secure the money for our construction. We had funds to start. Little by little, word got out about our project and we received help both financially and in free labor to strip down the old building and begin building with our new plans. Then something went wrong. Everything dried up. No more money or help came from anywhere. We had achieved nonprofit corporation status. We had succeeded in getting a zoning variance for our project. We had stripped out the old building and completed the framing and construction for our new youth center. We had proclaimed to the city and to the local churches what God was doing in this part of the neighborhood, and now ... nothing. God had turned off the spigot. I was devastated. How could God set me up like this? Was I a false prophet, proclaiming God's will for our project when actually it wasn't His will? Months and months went by while our project sat idle, and finally, I had to call the landlord and tell him, "Thank you for the offer of your building and for the funds, but we cannot proceed." I released him from his obligation to give us the building and quit.

I was so devastated that I could not even look at that building or drive past it. Years had gone into this project and my self-identity was even tied up in its success. Was God was punishing me for this? He was stripping away Michael Faber from the East Wind Youth Center. After all, I had been the driving force and visionary and legal architect of the project thus far. Eventually, I put it out of my mind. Then one day, the following year, I received a phone call from Dr. Hoang asking, "Michael, do you still want to do the Youth Center?" "Sure," I replied, "but we have no resources to complete the project." He told me not to worry, he had paid the additional $100,000.00 for construction himself. He would rent us the facility if we wanted to proceed. God had come through and provided us with a building!

We still had no staff and no money for operations. So I regathered what was left of our original group, now diminished by half, and we prayed for God's provision. It turned out, although we had quit, money had still been coming in to the Presbytery of Sacramento that was supporting us. We had seed money! But we still had no one to run the program. That night I attended a local political function with a friend, where I met a very interesting Asian man. As I spoke to him, I sensed the presence of the Holy Spirit in him, even though we had not mentioned religion. I asked him point blank, "Are you a Christian?" "Yes!" he replied. Then as two brothers in Christ, we spoke of his interests and my dreams. It turned out that he loved children, he loved music, he loved the LORD and most importantly, he was unemployed! The LORD had provided our first staff member. Mr. Minh Pham served as our initial director and helped us to establish our program.

As time went on, God also provided us with the people He wanted us to minister to. They were not the teenage gang members we had initially envisioned, but elementary and junior high school children whose parents needed free day care in that poor neighborhood. That was okay. God sent us the people He desired to hear of His love and to receive His mercy.

I wish I could report that from that day forward we lived happily ever after and that our program was strong even to this day. No, we choked along from week to week and month to month, always on the verge of financial collapse. We were never financially secure. We learned to rely on God's provision in the face of uncertainty. We learned to see each day of our program as a gift from God, since we were never sure that we would be around the following month. We knew we had to make each day count. Three years later, after some staff changes, we eventually had to close our doors. This was also extremely disappointing to me. At the end of our service, about 20 of our East Wind Youth Center kids came to Grace Presbyterian Church and sang the song, "Give Thanks." It still brings tears to my eyes. I realized that God used us to bring His love to all these children who otherwise would not know of Him. In my heart, I wished God would have provided more so we could keep the program open, but I learned to depend on God in adversity and to be thankful for whatever He gave. I was thankful to God for these children. I was thankful for the three years of ministry He gave to me and the entire team. I was thankful for those who accepted Christ as their personal Savior and for all the other seeds that we were allowed to plant. **God provided what we needed, not what we wanted. He gave us enough to do the ministry that He had planned, not what we had planned.**

I received another insight from this experience. We are not promised eternal life in this world. Everything must die. People die. Ministries die. Organizations die. God gives us provision for the time He allows us on this earth and nothing more. When provision ceases, it may be God's way of concluding the time He has given. Sometimes in poor places, the people of God die of hunger or starvation. In the First World we die of disease, heart attack, or violence. We all die, one way or the other. We do not have eternal life in this lifetime. God provides for us during the time He has given us. He gives us what we need for this time, but nothing more. It is a hard lesson, but one shown by our own experience.

JEHOVAH JIREH-HE PROVIDES A WAY TO ETERNAL LIFE

We all know the story of Abraham. God called him out of the land of Ur, and he went. God counted Abraham's faith as righteousness and promised that he would become the father of many nations and that through his descendants, the world would be blessed. But despite these promises, Abraham grew old with no children. We all know how Abraham tried to "fix things" and help God along, but how in reality, he only made a mess. Eventually, when Abraham was 100 and Sarah was 90, God came through on his promise and provided Abraham the long awaited son who would be his heir through Sarah. The boy's name was Isaac, meaning "he laughs," because God's timing was such that he provided a child to a couple whose bodies were as good as dead. As Isaac grew older, Abraham's faith surely increased as the boy survived and grew stronger. Then one day, God decided to test Abraham's faith by demanding that he sacrifice his only heir (he had already driven away Ishmael and his mother). Abraham responded to this horrible demand by taking his only remaining son up to the top of Mount Moriah as commanded by the LORD. We can only imagine the grief in his heart as the boy asked of him, "The fire and the wood are here, but where is the lamb for the burnt offering?" (Gen 22:7 NIV). He proceeded to take Isaac to the altar and then tie him there. He lifted his hand for the fatal blow, when an angel called out, "Do not lay a hand on the boy!" (Gen 22:12 NIV). Abraham was surely relieved, but still he needed a sacrifice and hadn't brought one. Then he looked up and there in a thicket, he saw a ram caught by its horns. The Bible records that he sacrificed the ram rather than his son. He then called that place "The LORD Will Provide" (Gen 22:14 NIV) or Jehovah Jireh as in the KJV alliteration. God provided a sacrifice where there was none.

God didn't just bring annual rain and bumper crops. In Abraham's case, He came through in an emergency. It is worth noting that while Abraham was prevented from sacrificing his beloved son to prove his love and devotion for the LORD, God followed through with the sacrifice of His only begotten Son, Jesus, on the cross, to prove His love for mankind. God provided His only begotten Son as sacrifice for the sins of all mankind, so that sins could be forgiven and our relationship restored. He provided a means of reconciliation, so that we would not lack or want the means to eternal life.

Michael L. Faber

GOD PROVIDES SATISFACTION, LOVE, JOY PEACE

God doesn't just come through for us with food and water, facilities, people, opportunities, and eternal life. He also provides us peace, joy, and satisfaction. Remember our earlier Scripture, Deuteronomy 16:15? God promised that when we thank Him and rely on Him, our joy will be complete.

This is supported by Proverbs 13:25. The righteous, those who are right with God, will eat to satisfy their souls. In contrast, the wicked experience want in their bellies. They are always hungry. When we follow God and have a relationship with Him, when we are filled with His Holy Spirit, we do not want. Rather we are filled to the point that our souls are satisfied.

Scientific studies show that people who attend religious services weekly find more life satisfaction and happiness than those who don't. Secularists claim that this is because people who go to church have activities and community. While this is true, even when comparing people with activities and community outside the church to people who attend church, those who go to church are happier. As the French philosopher Blaise Pascal stated, "There is a God-shaped vacuum in the heart of every man which cannot be filled by any created thing, but only by God, the Creator, made known through Jesus." St. Augustine wrote, "Thou hast made us for Thyself, O LORD, and our hearts are restless until they rest in Thee."

When we have a relationship with Christ, when we are trusting in the Good Shepherd, He fills the empty spot in our souls, and nourishes us where we are lacking. This may be physical or emotional nourishment, but often it is spiritual nourishment.

Now that we are in the new covenant, when we accept God's provision of eternal life by believing in His Son, Jesus Christ, we receive an even greater provision. He provides us with the Holy Spirit. When we are filled with the Holy Spirit and allow Him to work in our lives, we receive the fruit of the Spirit. In Galatians 5, Paul lists some of the fruits of the Spirit: These include love, joy, and peace. Unlike the Old Testament, where God was external to man, in New Testament, due to the death and resurrection of Jesus Christ, we can have the Holy Spirit actually live in us (Rom 8:9). We have the opportunity to be filled with the Spirit of Christ. The results of this filling include peace, joy and happiness.

Through the Holy Mass, Jesus, the Good Shepherd provides His body, blood, soul, and divinity to eat, and it nourishes and satisfies our soul.

When the LORD is our Shepherd, we do not lack. As we who seek righteousness by seeking the Master, trust in Him and follow Him, we indeed eat to our soul's satisfaction. Jesus promises us, "Blessed are those who hunger and thirst for righteousness, for they shall be filled" (Matt 5:6 NIV). Those who do not seek righteousness through God, those who do not trust in the LORD as their Shepherd, they will feel lacking in their bellies. They shall still want and crave more to satisfy their restless souls. They are ever seeking and never finding.

Thus we can conclude that when the LORD is our Shepherd, we shall not want. **We may have less than the wicked, but what God gives us will be sufficient.** He will meet our needs, physically, emotionally, and spiritually. He will give us joy and satisfaction through the power of His Holy Spirit.

QUESTIONS

1. When we read a Scripture that does not seem to be true, what should we do?

2. Does Psalm 23:1 promise us that God will give us everything we desire? If not, what does it promise?

3. How can we live abundant joyful lives when it seems that the faithful have less than the wicked?

4. Why does the Bible say the wicked go to bed hungry?

5. What might be a reason why so many faithful seem to struggle financially either individually or in their ministries?

6. If we "shall not want," why do some people in the world still starve to death or go bankrupt?

YOU LEAD ME TO GREEN PASTURES: ©Ann Ostini

2.

A GOD WHO GUIDES

"He maketh me to lie down in green pastures: He leadeth me beside the still waters" (Psalm 23:2 KJV)

Scripture says, "He makes me lie down in green pastures. He leads me besides still waters" (Ps 23:2 RSV). We see here a picture of a God who guides. There are many places that we might end up if left to our own devices. As people of God, however, we look to Him as our Shepherd and allow Him to lead us where He wills. He leads us to those places that are good for us and which nourish us physically and spiritually. Do you allow God to lead you in your life? How is it that you can discern His guidance for your life?

A GOD WHO PROVIDES

Like sheep, we need food. The psalmist says the Great Shepherd leads us to the green grass. The Hebrew word in this verse is *dashe* which actually means grass sprouts. These sprouts are fresh and green. These sprouts do not grow everywhere, but the Shepherd knows where the places with the green sprouts are and takes His sheep there. As sheep, we need water, so the Great Shepherd leads us to the still waters. Real sheep prefer to drink from places where the water is still rather than running. Perhaps they are afraid of the sound or are afraid they will drown if they fall into a flowing stream. But they are more at peace and more comfortable drinking from a place where the water is still. In our lives, there may be many things that we need, but because of our fears and prejudice and ignorance, we are not comfortable enough to receive those things. God knows what we need and He knows the circumstances under which we are able to receive what we need. Not only does He give us what we need, but He helps us to receive it. As discussed in the last chapter, God makes sure we have everything we need, even if we don't get everything we want!

A GOD WHO GUIDES

To get to our current theme, however, we must look beyond the places of the green pasture and the still waters, and instead look at the verbs the psalmist uses. He "makes" us to lie down, He "leads" us to the still waters. What we see here, is a God who is in control, and He is guiding us and taking us to the places we need to be. We all know that when we are His people, God guides us. The psalmist declares, "The steps of a man are established by the Lord, And He delights in his way" (Ps 37:23 NASB) When we delight in the way of the LORD and attempt to follow His way, He guides us, establishes our steps, and shows us where to go.

HOW DO WE DISCERN GOD'S GUIDANCE?

Many Christians rightfully say, "I want to be led by God, but I don't hear His voice when I pray" or "I can't tell if what I feel and hear is really from God or from myself." This is a common complaint, since God does not speak in an audible voice to the vast majority of us. What is the voice of God? Jesus says, "My sheep hear my voice" (John 10:27 RSV). Also Jesus says, "Whoever belongs to God hears what God says. The reason you do not hear is that you do not belong to God." (John 8:47 NIV). Wow!

Unfortunately, a great many Christians do not believe they have ever heard from God. Is it because they do not belong to Him or because they have not yet learned how to listen? I know a good number of people have heard from God, but they do not realize that God is speaking to them. Not every encounter with the voice of God is a Moses and the burning bush encounter! That story made it into the Bible because it was so spectacular. How do average Christians hear the voice of God? What does it sound like?

CHECK YOUR CONSCIENCE!

One of the easiest ways to get guidance from God is to check your own conscience. How many times have you been confronted with an opportunity to follow or a path to take, but in your quiet time you just have this feeling in your gut that something is not right? The very first thing we should check when seeking the will of God is our own conscience. Why is this? I call it spiritual instinct. God hardwires each of us with a basic sense of right and wrong. We can reprogram this instinct by deliberately and repeatedly acting against our conscience or through repeated reception of false teaching. This hardens our hearts to the whisper of the spirit. The catechism states it beautifully, "Deep within his conscience man discovers a law which he has not laid upon himself, but which he must obey. Its voice ever calling him to love and to do what is good and to avoid evil, sounds in his heart at the right moment…For a man has in his heart a law inscribed by God…His conscience is man's most secret core and his sanctuary. There he is alone with God whose voice echoes in his depths" (Catechism of the Catholic Church 1776).

The Jesuits have developed a prayer practice called the Examen. At the end of the day, they teach us to deliberately review the events of the day to see what actions and words we did that brought us joy, and what actions and words brought us a sense of unease. By setting aside a quiet time to review they day, we give ourselves a time alone within the secret core and sanctuary of the conscience to give the Spirit a chance to confirm or repudiate the paths we have been taking.

THE HOLY BIBLE

In trying to find the will of God for our lives, and in an attempt to hear His voice, another early step we must take is frequent consultation with the written word of God-the Holy Bible. In order for our conscience to work well in guiding our path, we must have a "well formed" conscience. "In the formation of conscience, the word of God is the light for our path; we must assimilate it in faith and prayer and put it into practice" (CCC 1785).

God spent thousands of years inspiring His prophets and speaking to His people so that His words could be written down and then preserved through the ages. The psalmist says of the Bible, "Thy word is a lamp unto my feet, and a light to my path" (Ps 119:105 RSV). When you are looking for direction, start with the Bible. With a little diligence, one can find the answers to a great many questions within the pages of the Holy Scriptures.

Often, when you are distressed or uncertain about a particular situation, the Holy Spirit will prompt your spirit with words directly from the Bible. Many people have found themselves in crises, when a verse that exactly fit the situation popped into their heads and gave them the support and direction they needed. Of course, this method won't work very well for you if you never pick up the bible, except to dust it. If you read the word of God regularly and hide His words in your heart, God will use the words stored in your memory banks and bring them to the screen of your conscious mind at just the right time. Apart from reading the Bible at home, you may hear the Scripture proclaimed at Mass or church. You may hear the words of God preached from the pulpit or the radio. The more you read and listen to the Scriptures, the more opportunities you give to the Holy Spirit to guide your steps through your daily life!

Of course, you need to be careful about using the Magic 8 Ball method of hearing from God through Scripture. Do you remember the Magic 8 Ball from the 1970s? You would ask a question, then shake the Magic 8 Ball, and then some vague answer would pop up to "answer" your question. Some people do the same with Scripture. They have some burning question in their heart, then randomly open the Bible and point to a Scripture, hoping that God's answer will be there. Perhaps you have heard the old joke where a seeker did this. He closed his eyes, opened his Bible, and pointed to a random Scripture. Opening his eyes, he saw Matthew 27:5 and read, "So Judas threw the money into the temple and left. Then he went away and hanged himself." The seeker shook his head and said to himself, "That wasn't very helpful." So he closed the Bible, reopened it, and with his eyes closed, pointed to another random Scripture. When he opened his eyes, they landed on Luke 10:37, "Jesus told him, 'Go, and do thou likewise.'"

I am sure that God did not desire this individual seeker to commit suicide, but when you start randomly opening Scriptures and pointing to verses, you never know what you will get! I recommend a different method. If the Holy Spirit is not bringing a verse directly to your mind, spend time in prayer and reading the Scriptures. Sometimes, the answer will jump out at you. As you are reading, some word or another will quicken your spirit and you may find God's word for you at this time.

A wonderful tool which helps with this is the ancient spiritual practice of *lectio divina.* In this exercise, you pray the Scriptures rather than studying them. You pick a passage and read it again and again deliberately and meditatively to ascertain the message that God has for you today. It is amazing how things can jump out at you and become clear through this practice. This is one way of hearing God's voice through the Holy Scripture.

SEEKING GODLY COUNSEL

Every Christian should gather around him or her several individuals who are known for their maturity, Bible knowledge, and life of prayer. Protestants may call these people mentors. Catholics may refer to them as spiritual directors. They do not have to be clergy! If you don't know anyone like this, you are probably hanging around with the wrong kind of people! In times of crises or uncertainty, share your heart with these people and ask for their prayers and guidance. Sometimes they will pray about your situation and share with you what they believe God is revealing to them about your situation. They may share wisdom from the Bible or their own common sense. "A wise man will hear and increase in learning, and the man of understanding will acquire wise counsel" (Prov 1:5 NASB). When you believe you have heard from God, it is also good to run what you believe you have heard passt these individuals, asking for their input. The Bible says, "Dear friends, do not believe every spirit, but test the spirits to see whether they are from God, because many false prophets have gone out into the world" (John 4:1 NIV). We are also reminded, "Do not treat prophecies with contempt but test them all; hold on to what is good" (I Thess.5:20-21 NIV). When we seek to hear directly from God on this issue or that as opposed to just studying the Bible to see what it says about an issue, we are seeking in the spiritual gift of prophecy. Prophecy is not predicting the future, but hearing the voice of God. If you believe you have heard the voice of the LORD about a particular matter, you should not hold this revelation in contempt or put it out of your mind, thinking it is crazy. Instead, you should test it to see if it is really of God. To test a prophecy, start by comparing it to Scripture. God will not tell you to sin (Jas 1:13). If the Bible says something is a sin, and you are hearing a voice telling you to do it anyway, you may be hearing from your own fleshly desires or a demon, or you may need mental health counseling. I had a friend who felt that God was telling him to steal women's underwear. Since the Bible clearly tells us that stealing is a sin, we can know, this spirit is not of God. Sometimes, when we are caught up in the moment and the excitement of our revelation, however, we do not see that the revelation is contrary to the Bible, which is why it is wise to seek counsel from other mature godly men and women of God who can help us test the spirit. "The way of a fool is right in his own eyes, but a wise man listens to advice," (Prov 12:15 RSV).

Just remember, our primary counsel must come from the LORD. "If any of you lacks wisdom, let him ask God, who gives to all men generously and without reproaching, and it will be given to him" (Jas 1:5 RSV). We seek counsel to help us understand and perceive the counsel of God, not to substitute their judgment for God's. Beware of letting others run your life or giving up your independent judgment in favor or another's, no matter how wise and mature they may be. Seeking counsel is a balance. It is a tool of a wise person for finding out and weighing the will of God. In the end, however, the final decision how you walk with the LORD must be yours.

CIRCUMSTANCES AND SIGNS

As we pray for God's guidance, we can also observe the circumstances and signs around us. We pray for God's guidance in our career, but while we may not hear a voice from God commanding us to "Take the job at Macy's," we learn to entrust our future to the LORD. We pray for His guidance and then depend on circumstances of open doors and shut doors to show us the way. We may apply for multiple jobs, and know that the ones that don't call us back were not meant to be, while others seem to miraculously open up for us. A wise Christian will pay attention to these signs while continuing to consult with Scripture. No, the bar tender job, the hit man job, or the nude dancing job are not of the LORD even if there is an open door. Wise Christians also seek godly counsel to understand these signs. What are others feeling about this move? They may look for other signs to back up the open door, or even set a fleece before the LORD.

Other signs may be other circumstances such as sudden closings of other opportunities or relationships that may have held us back from making the move, calls out of nowhere with words of encouragement, unexpected money, illness or tragedy. This may seem hit or miss, but when we believe that there is a Great Shepherd who is guiding us, and we combine together all the signs, signals, counsel, and Scripture, we often discover that they point a single way. We can have confidence that God is guiding our path.

WHAT IS A FLEECE?

In the book of Judges, the Bible tells the story of a young man named Gideon who was chosen by God to be the judge over the tribes of Israel and to rescue them from the oppression of the Midianites. At the time, the tribes of Israel were scattered and weak and Gideon was from one of the weakest tribes. When he heard the LORD say, "Go in the strength you have and save Israel out of Midian's hand," (Judg 6:14 NIV), Gideon was skeptical that this was really God speaking. He asked the LORD to give him a sign that it was really God speaking to him and not his imagination. God provided an initial sign that satisfied Gideon, then as the battle was about to commence, Gideon asked God to show that He was really on Gideon's side. Gideon suggested that he would place a wool fleece on the ground. In the morning, if there was dew only on the fleece but the ground was dry, he would know God was with him. The next morning, it turned out exactly as Gideon had suggested. Gideon still doubted, perhaps wondering if his "sign" was just a coincidence or the way things would happen naturally, so he begged the LORD's indulgence and requested that if it was really God's desire for him to face the Midianites, then the dew would only be on the ground and not the fleece the next morning. Of course, come next morning it was exactly as Gideon had suggested, and the boy knew God was with him. He conquered the Midianites and set his people free for a time. You can read the story yourself in Judges 6.

Individuals attempting to discern God's will have often used the method. They may have an inkling of what God is requiring of them, perhaps to seek someone's hand in marriage, change a career, go on a mission, but they are not sure they are making the right move. They want to know this is really God's will, so they "set a fleece before the LORD." They may pray something like, "If this is really you, God, make this or that thing happen to show me a sign." If the event happens, they feel confident that God is really in it. Sometimes, if the event doesn't happen, but they really want to do that particular thing, they set a different, perhaps easier test for God to perform, until they finally achieve the confirmation they desire. I have not personally used this method to obtain needed confirmation for my plans, because I have always thought it somewhat presumptuous to set up tests for God. Remember, just because someone did something in the Bible, we shouldn't necessarily think that what they did was good, or should be repeated, or is the standard for all of us to follow every time we desire to know God's will.

I have personally followed what Gideon did at first, saying, "How do I know this is really you? Please show me a sign." Then I let God choose the sign to show me. If I see the sign, I may feel confirmation in my heart, that I should proceed, confident that God is with me. Signs that I have personally experienced that gave me confirmation were the receipt of a $5,000.00 donation out of the blue which was exactly what I needed. Meeting exactly the right person to hire just when I needed that person, having a TV crew walk out just when I needed them and agreeing to do an interview just when I required it, and many other little things, none of which were miracles in themselves, but they were all things that happened just at the right time and just in the right amount to encourage me that God was with me in the task that I felt he was leading me.

HEARING THE VOICE OF GOD

So far, we have only spoken of very natural things in our attempt to hear from God. We check our conscience; we read the Bible; we consult with knowledgeable, godly people; we pay attention to events around us which may be signs from God; and perhaps we even set some conditions to test if a particular path is from God or not. These methods are the most common methods that believers attempt to hear from God, but they are not the only ways. Believe it or not, we can and do hear from God directly, if we will only listen! We must learn to recognize the voice of the Master. Jesus states, "My sheep hear my voice" (John 10:27 RSV). This is as true today, as it was 2000 years ago, when Jesus of Nazareth walked the earth.

It is not uncommon for a person who is prayerful and who waits upon the LORD to hear God respond. ***Prayer is not just a one way radio transmission, but more like a two way cell phone.*** We dial up God and tell Him our concerns, fears, and desires, but if we are not too quick to disconnect the call by saying "Amen," we may perceive a response. I use the word, "perceive" rather than "hear," because in my own experience, when God responds to me in my prayers, I do not hear His response with my ears, but rather hear His voice in my mind. Before I proceed to relate my personal experiences, I know some believers do not believe that people hear God's voice directly these days, so I would like to point to a few Scriptures, though I know it would take an entire book to discuss them all. This is a devotional book, not a theological thesis, so I will just mention a few.

First of all, Jesus states "My sheep hear my voice" (John 10:27 RSV). All of us who are believers are His sheep, and indeed, the LORD is our Shepherd. As His sheep, we hear His voice. Since the Shepherd guides us, not just into salvation, but throughout our lives, it is necessary to hear His voice, and Jesus says we will.

Second, according to Paul, if we belong the Christ the Spirit of God lives in us. (Rom 8:9). This very Spirit of God leads us, for "all who are led by the Spirit of God are the sons of God" (Rom 8:14 RSV). To be led by the Spirit implies that God (the Spirit is part of the Trinity) is communicating with us while leading us, and therefore must still be speaking to us. Paul goes on to state in that same passage, "it is the Spirit himself bearing witness with our spirit that we are children of God" (Rom 8:16 RSV). This shows that the Spirit of God which lives in us does communicate with us. I do not believe such communication is limited to assurance that we are God's children, since Paul makes it clear that the Spirit leads us in our walk with God.

The New Testament has numerous stories about individuals hearing God leading them to take particular actions in their lives. Paul certainly heard from Jesus on the road to Damascus. Ananias heard God telling him to go to Saul's address and heal him from his temporary blindness. Philip was shown where to go to encounter the Ethiopian Eunuch. On and on, story after story, we see God's people directed to go certain places and do certain things to advance the Kingdom. This is being led by the Spirit. Some may hear instructions from God to share a word with others. This is the gift of prophecy (See I Cor. 13).

In church history, there have been countless Saints who have heard God's voice, and seen visions, and received visitations of heavenly beings whether angels, Jesus, Mary, or other Saints. The Church holds open the possibility that God may choose to communicate in such exciting ways, calling it personal revelation.

What does the voice of God sound like? You will have to ask those who claim to have heard from God. For me, it is like a thought in my head that is outside my stream of thoughts and speaks to me in the 2nd person ("you") instead of the first person, ("I"). Once, after an enjoyable conversation with another person, I prayed saying, "Boy, that party was really fun." Immediately, I had the thought, "That is because you just were talking about yourself the whole night!" This thought was external to mine; it was contrary to my own desire, and yet it was consistent with Scripture or something God might say. He was chastising me for being self-centered. There have been many times in my life where God speaks to me and refers to Himself as "I" and myself as "You". In my last book, *Keys to a Happy Life: The Beatitudes According to Jesus*, I shared a story where God spoke to me while I was on Facebook and said "Make friends with that man." The man was a pastor from Kenya. I did so, despite some initial misgivings. Through that pastor, another pastor in India sought my friendship. Over the last five years, this pastor has translated a number of my books into Telugu and printed and distributed them in India. Thousands have read my writings in a foreign land because God "spoke" to me in a thought, "Make friends with that man," and I obeyed. Many of these incidents are too personal to share on these pages, but each time they come, they are as thoughts external to my own in a "voice" that speaks to me. They often comfort me in times of distress, or reveal to me things about myself and God's desire for my life or my family.

My mentor, Pastor William H. Goddard, wrote a fine book entitled, *The Seven Voices of God*. The book recounts how God spoke to him seven times in 63 years, giving him words of comfort and direction and once answering a prayer. In one of my favorite episodes, he was a young man, attending the First Baptist Church of Panama City, Florida, when a traveling evangelist gave the call for full time ministry. Engaged to be married and very happy with his Air Force career, he gripped the front of the pew in order to successfully avoid going forward. The next Sunday, the evangelist preached on a totally unrelated topic and gave a general call, but again he felt the urge to go forward and again began to resist. Then he heard the voice of God speak to him saying, "The longer you hold back, the less the call will be." He obeyed God's desire for his obedience and went forward that day to give his life to the service of the ministry. I am very happy he did so, or otherwise, I may never have become a preacher and certainly would not have written this book! How amazing are the results when we obey the voice of God.

Sometimes, God speaks to me in a prompting, but not in a voice. I may intend to do something and the God prompts me to bring in another person, add a different thing to my itinerary, or write a check to a particular ministry or cause. Obeying these promptings does not always yield a miracle story (that I know of), but who knows what benefit may result or what disaster may be avoided by obeying such a prompting? Often promptings that come to me are invitations to others to pray. In my law office, I often encounter clients who are suffering, and I know my clients come to me for legal help, and not spiritual help, but sometimes as they are talking, the Holy Spirit prompts me to offer to pray for them, and so far this offer has always been gladly received.

In 2015, I had been attending Catholic Church for over 30 years with my wife who was Catholic. I was a Baptist preacher. It was my practice at the time to take the Eucharist, despite Church teaching to the contrary, because (as I would say) "It was the Lord's supper and not Rome's!" I attended Mass because my wife made me, but at least I was going to enjoy communion. One day I was sharing one of my books with the deacon, and a man named Bob Laywell approached us and saw my book and asked for one. When he looked at the back of the book, he saw I was a pastor. Since he regularly served as an extraordinary Eucharistic Minister, he knew I took communion every Sunday. He then confronted me in a very direct (and it seemed to me) aggressive manner. It seemed that every Sunday he was in the front row and would glare at me while I went passed him in the communion line. Truly, I tell you, I began to hate that man.

While I was praying in the 24 hour Eucharistic adoration chapel, Bob Laywell came in to get the keys to lock up the bathrooms. I averted my glance and then the Holy Spirit spoke to me. "Make friends with that man!" I did not want to hear that, but I knew it must be from God because hate was not a Christian emotion and it is my practice to obey when the Spirit speaks. I also remembered the good things that happened the last time the Spirit said, "Make friends with that man." The next Sunday, I struck a conversation with him. He was receptive to my fig leaf and soon he began an all out campaign to convert me to Catholicism. He tried every apologetic trick in the book. "You will never convince me, Bob. I know a lot more about the Bible than you do!" I pridefully exclaimed.

Soon after this, I was on vacation and I awoke in the middle of the night in a cold sweat. Again and again, I heard a voice saying, "Stop preaching in the Protestant Churches and become a Catholic!"

"No way! It must be demons", I thought. "No way, am I going to become a Catholic." Fortunately, the voice was persistent. Every time I sat down in chapel during my Wednesday night hour of prayer, I heard the same thing. This went on for a whole year. During this time, Bob loaned me a video about the Virgin of Guadalupe that overcame some objections I had to Catholicism, then on New Years Day 2016, my Indian pastor friend sent me a Facebook text. "What is your decision." I gave up. "My decision is to obey the voice of God and become a Catholic." I asked Bob to become my sponsor in The Rite of Christian Initiation of Adults (RCIA) and went out of my way on Easter Sunday, the day after my confirmation, to let him give me the Holy Eucharist licitly. Now Bob is one of my best friends and we are partners in various ministries.

Three years later, I am very glad I decided to listen to God, to become friends with Bob and to join the Catholic Church. In many ways, the Church has helped me deepen my walk with God and to become a better Christian. I have had to stop preaching orally on Sundays for the time being, but God has opened many doors for me to teach his word and make an impact in people's lives. It is a good thing to obey the word of the LORD.

God indeed can speak to us directly, beyond the feelings of conscience, the general words of guidance found in Scripture, words of support from our mentors, or even signs and signals. He can speak if we will listen and life is exciting when we will open our ears to hear!

QUESTIONS

1. What are ways that you have heard the voice of God?
2. How can God speak to us through the Bible?
3. How can God speak to us through friends?
4. What should you do if you hear God tell you to do something that is a sin?
5. How might the practices of Examen or *Lectio Divina* help us to hear the voice of God?

3.

A GOD WHO GIVES BACK

"He restoreth my soul," (Ps **23:3 KJV**)

Psalm 23:3 has two parts, first. "He restores my soul" and second, "He guides me on paths of righteousness for His Name's sake." (NASB) This chapter, we will look at the first part. It is only four words in English and believe it or not only two words in Hebrew! But these two Hebrew words have a lot of meat, especially in our Christian faith walk.

Preachers throughout the ages have found it helpful to study the Scripture in the original languages, because often knowing the original language yields nuance and context which may not be apparent in translation. This is definitely the case with these two words. The literal meaning of the Hebrew word for "He restores" is "he returns" or "he gives back". The grammatical form of the word is an imperfect *polel*, which means that it is continuing, possibly repetitive, and intense. Thus, using the grammatical insight we obtain we could translate the phrase, "He continuously and enthusiastically gives back to us, possibly over and over, our "soul."

Now looking at the next phrase, "my soul," we find the Hebrew word used is *nefesh*. When we see the English word "soul" we think of our ghost or spirit which survives upon our death, but this is not really entirely what the word means in Hebrew. According to the Hebrew lexicon, the word *nefesh* has a number of meanings which we will explore.

WE ARE REFRESHED

According to Brown, Driver and Briggs, Hebrew and English Lexicon, the word *nefesh* means "seat of emotions and passions." Specifically, they suggest that the term "to give back the soul" or "give back the seat of emotions" could mean to refresh or cheer. NIV understands it this way, translating the verse, "He refreshes my soul." Note, they keep the idea of refreshing, while retaining the traditional translation of soul. David certainly could have meant it in this fashion. After all, he states the phrase right after saying that the LORD made him lie down in green pastures and led him beside still waters. When we are hungry, thirsty, and tired, food, water and rest, will certainly cause our spirits and our outlook to be refreshed. We will be cheered up. I am reminded of the story of the prophet Elijah, when he was fleeing from the wicked Queen Jezebel. Scripture records, "Elijah was afraid and ran for his life" (1 Ki 19:3 NIV). He ran into the desert and collapsed under a broom tree. He was so emotionally and physically exhausted that he actually prayed for his own death. God did not agree to that request and instead sent an angel who gave him a cake cooked over coals and a jug of water. He ate and drank and fell asleep. The angel returned a second time and saw that he ate and drank again so that he could be strengthened for his 40 day journey into the desert to meet God.

Because of his very real troubles, Elijah's spirit sunk to a level that he even prayed for death. God is a God who gives back, however, and the LORD ensured that Elijah had what he needed to regain his spirits and his strength. In that case, all he needed was rest, food, and water, the same things the shepherd gave his sheep in Psalm 23.

When our spirits sink, rather than wallowing in grief and pity, perhaps we should remember that the LORD refreshes our spirits. Eat something. Drink something. Relax and pray, "LORD, I know you refresh my soul. Please refresh my spirit now through your Holy Spirit. Give me peace. Give me a fresh Spirit. Restore my joy. Amen." Try that and see if you don't feel better right away.

Sometimes, life drags us down with extreme adverse circumstance and loss. Perhaps, food, water, and rest don't seem like enough. At one time or another, we all have crooned the old slave spiritual song, "Nobody knows the trouble I've seen," even though most of us only know the first line. The traditional lyrics go as follows:

> Nobody knows the trouble I've seen
> Nobody knows my sorrow
> Nobody knows the trouble I've seen
> Glory hallelujah!

Sometimes I'm up, sometimes I'm down
Oh, yes, Lord
Sometimes I'm almost to the ground
Oh, yes, Lord
Although you see me going 'long so
Oh, yes, Lord
I have my trials here below
Oh, yes, Lord
If you get there before I do
Oh, yes, Lord
Tell all-a my friends I'm coming to Heaven!
Oh, yes, Lord

Whatever our First World problems, few of us have had the amount of trouble endured by African American slaves prior to the Civil War. Yet, these slaves knew where to look when they started feeling low. They looked to the LORD and despite their physical troubles, they were able to shout, Glory Hallelujah! Now the slaves needed more than just some food, water and rest. They could eat and drink and maybe rest on Sunday, but come Monday, they were still subject to the injustices of slavery. How could their spirits be lifted? The song tells us, that besides the essentials of life, their faith gave them something else to lift their spirit, and that is hope. They had the Blessed Hope that no matter how bad things might be down here on earth, someday God would bring them Home to heaven. Elsewhere, the psalmist declares, "My soul, wait in silence for God only, For my hope is from Him. He only is my rock and my salvation, My stronghold; I shall not be shaken" (Ps 62:5-6 NASB).

No matter what life throws at you, no matter how mean and cruel others can be, we always have the choice of how we will react. Remember Paul and Silas singing as they were chained to a wall in prison? Paul declares, "For I am convinced that neither death, nor life, nor angels, nor principalities, nor things present, nor things to come, nor powers, nor height, nor depth, nor any other created thing, will be able to separate us from the love of God, which is in Christ Jesus our Lord" (Ro 8:38-39 NASB). No matter what physical or emotional thing this world or Satan can throw at us, we can be certain that God is our rock and our salvation. Nothing can separate us from His love, and nothing can deny our hope of eternal life with Him in the world to come!

I once had a friend named Dorothy. I first met her in court when her husband was getting a restraining order against her. Then I found out she was homeless and mentally ill. She was living out of her car. Due to the fact that I told her she could park in back of my office, I came to know Dorothy quite well as she lived on my property for 8 years. This was a woman who lost her mind, lost her husband, lost her money and lost her health. She eventually died of cancer. Despite this, every day, no matter what the day before her had brought, and no matter what arguments we had in the past, she would show up first thing in the morning bright and chipper, with a smile on her face. Even though she lost everything, she held on to one thing, and that thing was her faith in Jesus. She knew, really knew, that even if no one else seemed to love her, God loved her. Despite the tears and yelling that her internal mental illness brought her to, there was always a smile lurking beneath. Despite, her deranged ramblings, she could launch into the most eloquent testimony of her faith in God and how

God brought her comfort in her life. The LORD, indeed, did restore her soul!

We can choose. Wallow in pity or look to the LORD. No matter what the world brings you, God can bring you waters of refreshment and joy that bubbles from within. He restores my soul.

OUR LIVES ARE HANDED BACK TO US

While the context of Psalm 23 indicates that the word *nefesh* means "seat of emotions and passions" and that the LORD refreshes us with His comfort, the dictionary also says *nefesh* means soul (the traditional translation) or life. Specifically, *nefesh* is the breathing substance of being or the inner life. Note, in Jewish context, animals also have a *nefesh*. God breathes life into nostrils of the *nefesh* to make it a living being. In other words, in the Hebrew context, the *nefesh* is our life, our being, what distinguishes us from being a rock or a tree.

While not indicated by the context, the words of Psalm 23:3 state that "He returns my life to me" (repeatedly, and with intensity). Sometimes in Scripture, words take on meaning and context that weren't intended by the original author, but powerful meaning jumps out at future readers. In this case, isn't this a wonderful picture of what our God really does? "He returns my life to me (repeatedly, and with intensity). How often do we hand ourselves over to the slavery of sin and death? We become alcoholics, but the LORD delivers us. We join a gang and are owned by the forces of sin and destruction, but the LORD delivers us. We allow depression and sadness to overtake us and own us, and drag us to the pit of despair, but our Shepherd reaches down with His holy staff, pulls us up, and restores our joy. We become slaves to pornography, gambling, drugs, hatred, envy, jealousy, revenge, and anger. Again, our Shepherd comes through and delivers us! How does He deliver us? We voluntarily gave ourselves over to the mastery of the Evil One. We sold our souls to Satan for the momentary pleasures of sin, and yet our God is our rock and our salvation.

One of my favorite things to hear in church are testimonies. We don't do enough of that any more. Isn't it wonderful when a brother or sister stands up to share what God has done in their lives. We hear from the former alcoholic who groveled in his addiction, how he lost family, friends, and job. Perhaps he was out on the street. Perhaps he tried many times on his own to beat the addiction, but could not. Then one day, someone reaches out to him with the gospel, and he receives it. Then, with God's help and the help of his brothers and sisters in Christ, he is delivered, and his life is restored!

Then the sister stands up and shares how she always wanted love and affection and was willing to do anything for it. Perhaps she allowed herself to be used and abused sexually, and then to numb her shame, she turned to drugs. Now, needing money for drugs, she turned to prostitution. A drug addicted prostitute was what she was. Then someone shared the gospel with her and she was born again. With help and hard work, she beat her addiction and Jesus restored her life and now she is productively employed, perhaps even married with family. God gave her life back to her! Testimony time is so powerful because we see God at work changing lives and doing miracles in our hearts.

We know the story. "While we were yet sinners, Christ died for us" (Ro 5:8 RSV). Through His blood we were redeemed, bought, and purchased. The price for our sin was paid. "In Him we have redemption through his blood, the forgiveness of our trespasses,, according to the riches of his grace which he lavished on us" (Eph 1:7-8 RSV). In other words, because of God's great mercy, He paid the price for our sins through the shedding of His blood. Because the price of sin has been paid, we can be forgiven.

When we were baptized, "We were therefore buried with him through baptism into death in order that, just as Christ was raised from the dead through the glory of the Father, we too may live a new life" (Rom 6:4 NIV). Jesus, the Good Shepherd, rescues us from slavery to sin, takes our lives from the Devil and gives them back to us! He does this theologically, at the moment of salvation, and practically, every time we backslide and fall into sin but then upon realizing it, call to Him for help.

In the Catholic Church, we have the wonderful sacrament of confession. We know that Jesus is in the forgiveness business. No matter how we have messed up, no matter how deep or long standing the sin, we can always go to the Church and meet with a priest, who is a duly appointed agent of the Bishop, who is a successor to the original apostles. Speaking to his apostles Jesus delegated to them the power of forgiveness of sin. After His resurrection from the dead, He gathered his apostles together, prior to Pentecost and breathed on them, giving them a special spiritual gift. Jesus said to them, "Receive the Holy Spirit. If you forgive the sins of any, they are forgiven; if you retain the sins of any, they are retained" (John 20:21-23 RSV). Prior to this, while healing the paralytic, Jesus used his power to forgive sins as evidence that He was God. "But so that you may know that the Son of Man has authority on earth to forgive sins" (Matt. 9:6 NASB). Now he delegates this authority to His apostles who in turn delegated it to the bishops and their priests. When a priest hears a confession, he hears it on behalf of Christ, and uses power delegated to him by Christ, to speak Christ's words, "Your sins are forgiven."

"The sacrament of Reconciliation with God brings about a true "spiritual resurrection," restoration of the dignity and blessings of the life of the children of God, of which the most precious is friendship with God" (CCC 1468). Faithful practice of this sacrament leads to "an increase of spiritual strength for the Christian battle" (CCC 1496).

Christians who struggle with sin may find restoration by having the humility to think about how they have sinned, to be sorry for their sins, and humble enough to confess these sins out loud to a priest. The priest, listening on behalf of Christ, suggests a penance and then pronounces the words of absolution. The discipline and humility required to practice this confession is of great benefit to the Christian struggling against the vices of repetitive sin. God understands, hears, forgives, and gives grace to avoid recommitting the sin.

You would think that we only would need rescuing once, yet given the war being waged in our bodies between the laws of sin and death and the spirit of life, we often forget our first love and fall back into the lure of sin. While this is painful to the LORD and to us and our loved ones, as we reap the consequences of this repeated sin, but when, like the Prodigal Son, we finally come to our senses, we always have the privilege to turn away from our sin and turn back to our Heavenly Father, who will forgive us and rescue us once again from the clutches of sin. Any of you who are recovering addicts or who struggle with besetting sin know this cycle. What a privilege to have a Heavenly Father of whom, as the Apostle John can declare, "If we confess our sins, he is faithful and just and will forgive our sins and purify us from all unrighteousness" (1 John 1:9 NIV). As we confess our sins to our LORD, He bestows upon us the benefits of fresh forgiveness. We may have been forgiven at the moment of salvation, but as we confess, we attain for ourselves in that temporal moment the benefits of forgiveness already granted. In other words, we feel it. God then supernaturally helps us to break the bonds of sin and overcome its hold on us, so that if we keep looking to Him, we will not be required to keep returning to our sin. We need that supernatural help, because we cannot do it on our own.

I have friends who have suffered from alcoholism and drug addiction. Through their faith, Jesus delivered them from that addiction and gave their lives back to them. These individuals did not necessarily never touch alcohol again, or even never get drunk again. They have "fallen off the wagon," but they never were held hostage by their addiction again. They were never slaves to it, and through the help of Christ, they were able to move up and move on and become productive members of society, because the Great Shepherd returned their life to them with intensity and with joy.

QUESTIONS

1. When faced with depressing circumstances, how might we use Psalm 23:3 to regain our composure.

2. Is the refreshment of God a one time event?

3. Share a story of how God refreshed your spirit after an adverse circumstance.

4. Have you had an experience where God literally gave you back your life?

5. Has the practice of confession helped you overcome a particular sin?

4.

A GOD WITH A REPUTATION TO KEEP

"He leadeth me in the paths of righteousness for his name's sake" (Ps 23:3 KJV)

As our Shepherd, the LORD has provided for us in times of need and taken us to the good places. He has led us to the places of food, water, and rest. We have learned that we can expect to hear His voice to guide us in our lives and our careers and to help us with our decisions. He even provides spiritual refreshment and deliverance when necessary. All of these things have been for our benefit. While the LORD desires to guide us into the happy places, He also has expectations and desires for Himself.

He desires that we follow Him. He desires that we obey Him. He desires that we conduct our lives in a fashion that is worthy of His name. The second half of Psalm 23:3 says, "He leads me on paths of righteousness, for his name's sake" (ESV).

Believe it or not, how we live our lives affects the reputation of God. We can hurt His reputation and the reputation of those of others seeking to follow Him by calling ourselves Christian and then leading shameful lives. We can through our shameful decisions even prevent others from deciding to follow the LORD in the first place. Think about all the harm the recent sexual and financial scandals of Catholic and Protestant clergy have done to the cause of Christ. How many dismiss the teachings of Christ now, due to the failure of His followers?

PATHS *OF RIGHTEOUSNESS*

The psalm says He leads us in paths of righteousness. The word for path in Hebrew is "*ma 'egly*" which has a meaning something like ruts, or well-worn trenches cut into the ground from long use. You may have seen deer trails out in the forest. I have some in my backyard, leading straight from the break in our back fence right up to my wife's rose bushes. When the deer repeatedly travels in the same direction to the same place, the vegetation gets trampled and the ground compacted, so that a nice easy-to-follow trail is formed. The ruts are formed from longstanding use over and over again. Once formed, these ruts can be quite long lasting. It is still possible to go into desert places out west and see the ruts of the wagon trains carved into the prairie floor.

God leads us on similar ruts or paths of righteousness. He does not reinvent the wheel, or change what He considers righteous for each generation. Those in the world who reject God's word are constantly redefining what is right and what is wrong to fit the whims of each generation. "Don't be so old fashioned!" they declare. They can do this because they have no foundation other than what seems good and popular at the time. Rather than looking down to past generations and holy Scripture to seek a firm foundation of morality, they look sideways to what everyone else is doing for their stability. Elsewhere, the psalmist declares, "Thy word is a lamp unto my feet and a light unto my path" (Ps 119:105 KJV).

God's word is stable. It is a firm foundation. It is with His word as recorded in the Bible that he can lead us on paths of righteousness, so that we can feel secure that we are going the right way. His word is a lamp unto our feet, even when the world around us is dark and confused. Once I was in chapel, and I heard God speak these words to me, "A little light dispels a lot of darkness." With the advancement of technology and information, one would think that things would become clearer with all the extra information available. But instead, they seem more uncertain and muddier. Everyone has a theory; everyone has an opinion. With the increased number of voices in our heads and information available at our fingertips, it seems that nothing is certain anymore. Confusion is on the rise. Men don't know if they are male or female. Killing babies is something to be proud of. Declaring God's word is true is considered bigoted. Marriage rates are dropping as girls try to win the affection of boys through sex and call it women's rights. Society has chopped the strong ropes that once held us firm to the wharf of God's word and now our ship is drifting on the dark ocean and the waves are getting higher. A little lamp in a guard house back at the wharf a long distance away can yet be seen through this great darkness. It is the word of God. Will we return to it or continue our drift into the darkness of confusion?

The Bible says, "Jesus Christ is the same yesterday and today and forever" (Heb 13:8 NIV). Elsewhere it declares, "Heaven and earth will pass away, but my words will never pass away" (Mark 13:31 NIV). In other words, no matter what is happening in the world or even the universe around us, God's word is forever. His standards are unfailing. What are those standards? They are set forth in the word of God, the Holy Bible.

PATHS OF RIGHTEOUSNESS

If you compare, Bible translations, you will see some English translations translate Psalm 23:3 as "paths of righteousness", "right paths", "paths of justice" and one Jewish translation "straight paths". All of these could be correct. The Hebrew word *Tsedek*, contains all of these connotations. After all, paths in and of themselves have no moral value, but the phrase is a metaphor for a life style which God wants us to follow. He wants us to pursue *righteousness,* the state of being right with God. How can we be right with God? We start by believing in His Son Jesus Christ as LORD and Savior. (John 6:29). We follow this by active discipleship (i.e. avoiding sin and doing justice). Martin Luther taught, that to be fully human, we need to be right with God and right with man. To do this, we must perform the two acts of righteousness, *coram deo* and *coram mundi* (in the presence of God, and in the presence of the world). According to Luther, to be righteous before God, we only need faith in His Son Jesus Christ. However, in light of that faith, we should follow the guide of the law and show justice and mercy to those around us. Catholics see justification, or being right with God as a twofold path as well. "Justification establishes cooperation between God's grace and man's freedom. On man's part it is expressed by the assent of faith to the word of God, which invites him to conversion, and the cooperation of charity with the prompting of the Holy Spirit who precedes and preserves his assent" (CCC 1993). Thus, either way you look at it, true righteousness (being right with God) requires both faith and action.

Righteousness is not just having faith and avoiding sin. It is also showing mercy. Joseph was accounted to be a righteous man, which led him to want to put away Mary quietly when he thought she was guilty of adultery. He did not want to accuse her publicly, which could have led to her death. He showed her mercy as a fruit of his righteousness.

Finally, in the Hebrew, to be righteous, is to be straight. A righteous path is a straight one. There are no twists and winds and dangerous turns, but the road is straight and level. This is how our lives should be. A life lived in accordance with the will of God is a safe life and a good life. It is most likely to lead to long life and true happiness, both now and in eternity. This makes sense, when one considers that the Hebrew word for wickedness is "*avon*" which means to be twisted.

Satan loves to take that which is straight and twist it so that it points into a direction that the Maker never intended. See how he does this with our values, our views on family and sexuality, our culture, our music, and even the word of God itself! God does not want us to be twisted, he wants us to walk the straight path; the righteous path. "For God is not *a God* of confusion but of "peace" (1 Cor 14:33 NASB).

FOR HIS *NAME'S SAKE*

Much of the time, when I am teaching and writing, or back when I was still preaching, I am trying to convince my readers or congregation that following the path of righteousness is what is good for them. When we follow the LORD, we will be happy; we will be healthier. We may live longer. Our marriages will last longer. One of the things they do at St. Mel's Catholic Church every month is ask those who have an anniversary to stand up say their names and how long they have been married. Then everyone claps and the priest gives them all a blessing. I am constantly amazed at the number of people who have been married 50, 60, even 70 years. You would not see so many lengthy marriages in a secular group this size. This is the result of living godly lives and putting Christ first. But it is also a testimony to the truth of the gospel.

In the Bible, we see again and again that God is often motivated to help us for His Name's sake, rather than our own benefit. When the people of Israel rebelled against God in the desert, Moses argued for mercy towards the rebels not for their own sake, but because of God's own name. After all, Moses argued, everyone knows you did great miracles to lead us to the desert. They know of the promises you made to Abraham, Isaac, and Israel to multiply their seed. What would they think if you did all this just to kill us here? (Exodus 32:7-14). The implication is that they would think that God did not keep His word, or that He was unable to rescue His people. Through the prophet Ezekiel, the LORD, Himself admits, "for the sake of my name I did what would keep it from being profaned in the eyes of the nations" by preserving His rebellious people rather than destroying them" (Ezek 20:13-14).

In other words, in the larger scheme of things, preserving the reputation of the LORD is more important than our own temporary comfort and benefit. The Bible even states that "he chose us in Him before the creation of the world…to the praise of his glorious grace" (Eph 1:4-6 NIV) We were saved and marked with the Holy Spirit "to the praise of his glory" (Eph 1:13-14 NIV). In other words, our entire salvation (just as Israel's salvation) was for the praise of God's name and His glory, not our own personal benefit. What does this mean? We need to be living our lives for the glory of God's name, not our own personal pleasure or desires. Living God's way is of great personal benefit, but we don't do that for us alone, but also to fulfill our responsibility to God's holy name.

When we live out our faith walk, we are not only heaping God's blessings upon ourselves, but we are testifying to the world that God is real and that He has a real impact in our lives. In a sense, we are representing Christ to those around us. We are His ambassadors. Or as Paul says, "Or do we need, like some people, letters of recommendation…? You show that you are a letter from Christ, the result of our ministry, written not with ink but with the Spirit of the living God, not on tablets of stone, but on tablets of human hearts" (2 Cor 1-3 NIV). We are letters of recommendation. Paul said we, his readers, were Christ's letters of recommendation to others about the truth of what He was preaching. Paul didn't need a formal letter of recommendation from Jesus, or Peter or from the Council of Jerusalem to tell others he was a legitimate preacher. If someone wanted to know his credentials, he could point to the Church at Corinth and say, "See these people! This is proof of the truth of what I am preaching. This is proof that Jesus has blessed my ministry, because these people are living lives that reflect Christ."

When I attended RCIA, there was a beautiful young Asian lady in my class. She was there with her mother in law, Cathy. She had been married to Cathy's son for many years, but she was Buddhist and never saw the need to convert to Christianity. Cathy's husband had died a year or so earlier, and when this young woman saw how Cathy dealt with her grief with the peace that comes from true faith, she was convinced! She received her baptism the same year I was confirmed. Words could never convince her, but Cathy's actions were the testimony she needed to see.

As the old saying goes, "We are the only Bible that some people may ever read!" Our lives are a living testimony to the power of the gospel. As followers of the Living God, our lives reflect His nature, His goodness, and His reality to others. He guides us in paths of righteousness for His name's sake, because if we claim to be His children and live like the Devils' children we are harming the LORD's street cred.

In other words, how we live reflects on how true God's word seems to those around us. Every time a priest is caught molesting a child, or a pastor is caught having an affair or embezzling money, this action harms the entire church, and it harms the spread of the gospel. When the church's sexual scandals broke, even my faith was shaken. "Doesn't God have the power to change even His clergy and prevent them from such twisted actions?" the devil whispered in my ear. It really bothered me until I considered my own sin which I struggled with. While not as scandalous, it still kept popping up. I also considered a few other things not addressed by the media.

Priests hear the confessions of the entire congregation, and in essence take upon themselves all the ick of their parishioners. The person confessing walks away feeling light and forgiven, but the priest, standing in the place of Christ, has had more nails pounded into his hands and feet. This has to have some psychological effect. Second, what greater victory can Satan have than having a priest or pastor fall sexually. It creates a scandal. It is always newsworthy. The sin hurts not only the priest and the victim, but resounds across the nation and the world as the press gleefully shows yet another example of why the Church can't be trusted. When I was young and thinking about joining the Army, my dad told me, "Don't join the artillery. If you do, every gun on the battlefield will be aimed at you. In battle, everyone's goal will be to kill you first! It is better to be a rifleman." Sound advice. The same must be true in our spiritual battle. Every demonic gun is aimed at the priest. All the powers of hell are zeroed in on making him fall. This doesn't excuse the gravity of the crime or the tragedy of the fall both for the victim and the priest but does seem to explain why so many do fall.

The secular news media doesn't write a front-page story every time the church goes and hands out blankets to the homeless, or every time a Christian helps an elderly person with chores, or drills a fresh water well in Africa. News of those events must travel slowly, by word of mouth, but when people hear and see this kind of news, they give praise to God. These physical works of mercy are done to the betterment of God's reputation.

When I argue with atheists on the internet, they often seem to get the better of me if we are sticking to simple physical or scientific proof of God's existence. But where I start to win is when I can point to how Christians live and give and love. Unfortunately, to make my point, I must distinguish between Christians who actually live to follow the Bible and the teachings of the Church, and those nominal Christians who say they believe in God but do little to prove it. These Christian in name only undermine my attempts to spread the gospel, because the atheists can say, "See, they live just like everyone else. Believing in God makes no difference in their lives." My friend, Pastor Billy Crone, used to preach about Christians who lived no differently than the world, calling them "practical atheists." In theory, they believe in the existence of God, but practically, they live as though He does not exist! Jesus denounced these types of Christians in His letter to the church of Laodicea. "I know your deeds, that you are neither cold nor hot. I wish you were either one or the other! So because you are lukewarm—neither hot nor cold—I am about to spit you out of my mouth" (Rev 3:15-16 NIV)!

When Christians live according to the teachings of Christ, we make the most impact. When we live according to the customs of the world is when we do the most harm. Nonbelievers may not believe in our God, but they are impressed by our love. They will know we are Christians by our love. "By this everyone will know that you are my disciples, if you love one another" (John 13:35 NIV). They may not buy our theology, but they respect our lives. Little by little, the Holy Spirit will use this respect to gain a hearing for our faith. On the flip side, no one likes a hypocrite. When they know what our faith teaches, but see us acting as they do, they do not like us more, but rather respect us less, because we are not living according to our own standards.

The psalmist declares, "He leads me in paths of righteousness, for His name's sake" (Ps 23:3 ESV). For the sake of God's Name, for His reputation, and for the effectiveness of the Gospel, we must follow the paths of righteousness which He leads us to!

QUESTIONS

1. What is the best source for determining right from wrong?

2. Should morality change with the times? Does it? What causes this?

3. What are some things you could do to give God a better reputation?

4. Why do you think so many priests have fallen into sexual sin with children?

5. What is an extremely effective way to evangelize? Can we do it with actions alone?

THY ROD AND STAFF: ©Rob Rivera

5.

A GOD WITH US

"Yea, though I walk through the valley of the shadow of death, I will fear no evil: for thou art with me; thy rod and thy staff they comfort me" (Ps 23:4 KJV).

As the old song goes, "I beg your pardon, I never promised you a rose garden ... along with the sunshine there's gotta be a little rain sometimes." Experience shows us that our lives are full of good and bad. Or as the sage of Ecclesiastes declares, "There is a time for everything, and a season for every activity under the heavens" (Eccl 3:1 NIV). So often in the West, we have used technology and money to insulate ourselves from much suffering, but the truth is, no matter how blessed we are, no matter how rich we are, no matter how educated we are, we will still suffer sickness, disappointments, heartache, and eventually death. No matter how hard we try, evil in this world and the powers of sin and death will touch us and break our hearts. It might be the death of a loved one, the unfaithfulness of a spouse, the rebellion of a child, or the betrayal of a friend. Perhaps some accident or some disease will cause us pain and limitation. "There's gotta be a little rain sometimes."

WE ALL ARE GOING TO BE IN THE VALLEY

Sometimes, bad teaching in the body of Christ, leads us to believe that if we have enough faith, God will protect us from all harm and bless us materially so that we never suffer. God does bless us, and He does provide (as we discussed in the first chapter of this book), but trouble and hardship also come our way, just as it did for all the saints of God who preceded us. Christ Himself had no place to lay His head and He suffered persecution, rejection, physical suffering, and death. Paul learned to be content whether in need or whether in plenty. (Phil 4:11-12). He also suffered persecution, hardship, and death. Not all of us will know poverty, especially if we live in a wealthy country and make wise choices in our education and careers, but all of us will suffer other hardships, both physical and emotional. Eventually, our bodies will fail and we will be re-united with Christ. The question is not if we will suffer, but when and how.

The place described in this Psalm is "the valley of the shadow of death." W. Phillip Keller, in his famous book, *A Shepherd*

Life in the Good Shepherd's Flock: Meditations on Psalm 23

Looks at Psalm 23, describes how in the summer shepherds commonly drive their sheep from the lowlands up to green pastures high in the mountains. He states that the best route to drive the sheep from the lowlands up to the highlands is through the valleys carved out by streams and rivers. He wrote, "Every mountain has its valleys. Its sides are scarred by deep ravines and gulches and draws. And the best route to its top is always along these valleys." If you have ever walked on a trail in a mountain valley, you will have noticed that typically there are high mountain walls on either side of you which lurch over you and often block the sun, creating the shadows mentioned by the psalmist. Often, there is a rushing stream which carved the valley in the first place. Sheep do not care for rushing water and the sound scares them. This is why they prefer the shepherd to lead them to still waters to drink. This environment of darkness and sound and rushing water could certainly be stressful for a sheep. We humans are also often afraid of darkness and shadows, because we do not know what dangers might lurk behind them. It brings up inside us a primal fear of the unknown. The psalmist builds on this fear in his imagery by calling the dark place the "valley of the shadow of death." We are afraid of death because it is the greatest unknown. All together, the psalmist paints a picture of a place real or figurative of fear and uncertainty. We have all been in such places in life. Maybe it was the loss of a job, diagnosis of cancer, or the loss of a supporting loved one through death or divorce. Maybe it is creeping Alzheimer's or disability of some other type that grips our heart with fear as we face an uncertain and increasingly bleak future.

Notice that the Psalmist declares, "Yea, though I walk through the valley of the shadow of death…" (Ps 24:3 KJV) he does not say, if I walk through. We all will walk through the Valley sometimes; some of us walk through it many times in our Christian lives. He says, though I walk through. The word "though" sets up a situation that expects to soon experience a contrast. It is natural when we are in the dark places of our lives to suffer disappointment, despair, anger, and even fear. We know this is true because we have all been there and these feelings are the natural feelings of our flesh. The psalmist announces, however, that even when he is in such a situation, he will struggle against these natural feelings of the flesh, and instead, in his words, "I will fear no evil, for thou art with me" (Ps 23:4 KJV).

I WILL FEAR NO EVIL

In this psalm, the writer takes the voice of the sheep. The little lamb might be afraid for the environment around him, but he takes comfort in the presence of the Good Shepherd. We can identify with the little lamb as we face our valleys of the shadow of death. We can allow fear, anger, or a host of other negative emotions to take control, or like the psalmist, we can take comfort in the presence of our God.

Notice, the Scripture does not declare that the Shepherd will take him around the valley or over the valley or under the valley. Rather, walking through the valley is what will naturally happen, but through all of it, we need not fear, because the eternal Thou, our LORD, is with us. Christ sometimes delivers us from adversity through miraculous intervention, but often He is simply **with** us, through it all. Even His name, Immanuel, promises this faithful presence, since it means, in Hebrew, "God with Us."

We are all familiar with the famous poem, *Footprints in the Sand.* It goes like this,

Footprints in the Sand

One night I dreamed a dream.
As I was walking along the beach with my Lord.
Across the dark sky flashed scenes from my life.
For each scene, I noticed two sets of footprints in the sand,
One belonging to me and one to my Lord.

After the last scene of my life flashed before me,
I looked back at the footprints in the sand.
I noticed that at many times along the path of my life,
especially at the very lowest and saddest times,
there was only one set of footprints.

This really troubled me, so I asked the Lord about it.
"Lord, you said once I decided to follow you,
You'd walk with me all the way.
But I noticed that during the saddest and most troublesome times of my life,
there was only one set of footprints.
I don't understand why, when I needed You the most, You would leave me."

He whispered, "My precious child, I love you and will never leave you
Never, ever, during your trials and testings.
When you saw only one set of footprints,
It was then that I carried you."

- by Anonymous

In the poem, the author felt alone at the worst times of her life, only to later learn that it was Jesus carrying her along during those perilous moments. While this poem is quite inspirational, the sad point that it reveals is that many times during our most painful and perilous trials, we fail to discern the LORD's presence with us!

It is been said that one of the best marks of our character is not how we behave and react to success, but how we behave and react to failure and trials. Indeed, while I discern dangers to our faith under either circumstance, trials and testings indeed are the times that we find out if our faith is real. Will we react in the flesh to our adversity or will we remember that God is with us and put our trust in Him? It is exactly in the worst of times that our faith must prove of the most use to us. Our flesh will fear, but when we remember that God is with us, we receive His supernatural peace! Indeed, the Bible declares, "For God hath not given us the spirit of fear; but of power, and of love, and of a sound mind" (2 Tim 1:7 KJV). Our faith is most real when we do not follow the leadings of the flesh in adverse circumstances, but rather follow the direction of the Spirit. Over and over, the angels in the Bible declare, "Fear not!" The LORD is with us.

GOING THROUGH THE VALLEY IS FOR OUR BENEFIT AND OTHERS AS WELL

As noted above by W. Phillip Keller, the best way to get from the lowlands to the high mountain pastures is through the valleys. We all desire to be close to God and mature in our faith, or in Catholic terminology, to "achieve sainthood." At least I hope we do. But just as an athlete cannot achieve athletic prowess and victory without grueling training which includes painful punishing training and great discipline, neither is the path to spiritual maturity an easy one.

St. Peter wrote, "For this very reason make every effort to supplement your faith with virtue, and virtue with knowledge, and knowledge with self control, and self-control with steadfastness, and steadfastness with godliness, and godliness with brotherly affection, and brotherly affection with love" (2 Peter 1:5-7 RSV). St. Peter outlines a path of spiritual growth which he asserts will "confirm your call and election" (2 Peter 1:10 RSV). We begin with faith and grow and grow to our goal of love, but this path also includes the quality of steadfastness, or in other translations state, patience or endurance. In order to develop the quality of steadfastness, (or patience or endurance), one must have a trial, a test, or an irritant. No one likes trials, and we may certainly pray, as our LORD did, for the cup to be taken away, but in the end God may decide to allow these adverse conditions to remain to help us grow. As we face our trials, we learn to trust that God is with us in the midst of our personal valley of the shadow of death. While initially we often react to adversity with a "woe is me!" spirit, in time we learn that others (including the LORD and the saints who preceded us) also have had adversities and we can learn to move on in spite of our trials and tribulations. Sometimes we can, with God's help, turn our troubles into a strength. One of the most inspiring preachers I heard in my youth was a man that could barely talk because of his advanced condition of cerebral palsy. His name is David Ring. But in spite of his disability, God turned him into a wonderful preacher, inspiring others not give up when facing adversity, but instead but to seize it and overcome it. His motto was, "I have cerebral palsy. What is your excuse?" He was able to take a debilitating condition and use it as a tool for the glory of God. Likewise, in our suffering, we learn faith and courage. We learn through suffering that life is not always comfortable and easy. We can use these times to discipline the flesh.

There is a Catholic teaching on suffering that is quite interesting. It begins with the premise that Christ suffered bodily for our benefit. It follows that premise with the idea that we Christians who constitute the church are part of the actual body of Christ. (Eph 1:23). Therefore, as part of His body, we can offer up our suffering as an act of worship, joining it to His, for the benefit of others. Paul seems to indicate that this is exactly what he did on behalf of the church. "Now I rejoice in what I am suffering for you, and I fill up in my flesh **what is still lacking in regard to Christ's afflictions**, for the sake of his body, which is the church" (Col 1:24 NIV). Suffering can take on mystical meaning if you think of it in this way. You might object to this Scripture by saying, "Christ's sacrifice was sufficient." Yes, it was sufficient for reconciliation with God, but Scriptures make no secret of the fact that the children of God will suffer a great deal as they take the good news of Jesus out to the world, and live according to the dictates of our faith. This suffering which has been and will be done by the body of Christ through His people is what St. Paul speaks of in "what is still lacking in regard to Christ's afflictions." Furthermore, this suffering has occurred and still needs to occur in order to make the work of Christ effective by helping it reach all people. Therefore, when we offer our sufferings to Christ, we participate with Him in His saving work of bringing all to reconciliation with God. "Well," you may continue to object, "my personal suffering in sickness or family or financial problems have **nothing** to do with the spread of the gospel, therefore they cannot compare to what Paul was speaking about!" You think not? The earliest Christians suffered martyrdom! The way they faced that public suffering with courage and peace brought many to Christ. Likewise, when you face adversity in calmness of spirit and depth of faith, you can have great impact on the unbeliever, because he knows how **he** would have responded under like circumstances. Remember the young Buddhist lady inspired to Christian faith by the suffering of her mother-in-law after the loss of her husband. How the mother-in-law suffered was instrumental in planting the seed of faith in the daughter-in-law. The key is uniting your inevitable suffering to Christ and letting the Holy Spirit use it as a witness to the weak and the unbelieving. We may have the power to do this when we know that God is **with** us through these harsh times. In this way, we can add our suffering to His "for the sake of the church."

THROUGH THE VALLEY

While we cannot avoid the valley and every one of us will experience it, notice that the Scripture does not say that you are with me while I dwell in the valley of the shadow of death, forever. No. It says, "Yea, though *I walk through* the valley of the shadow of death, thou art with me" (Ps 23:4 KJV). Just as the Western shepherd, must take his sheep through the valley to get to the high mountain green pastures, so God takes us through the difficulties to get to a higher plane. Yes, there are lessons to be learned during our valley times, but they are preparing us for something ahead. We are meant to get through the valley onto our final destination. Yes, you may be in the valley right now. Stop despairing and **keep**

walking. Some of the greatest political heroes of the 20th century like Nelson Mandela and Gandhi and Martin Luther King, spent time in prison, so did the Apostle Paul back in the First century. These heroes were trained and hardened in these times for the struggles that lay ahead. God had better plans for them. Yes, they struggled and probably despaired, but God knew what was ahead and used their adversity to mold them.

"Well," you object, "What if I die in that valley?"

Unfortunately, some people do. We are not all rescued from our hard times. We do not all see a victorious time in this life that is the culmination of all of our struggles. Some just die without seeing it. This is not the end of their stories, however. We are saved into eternal life, and our experiences and our struggles are bound to have meaning in the afterlife. God is training us for heaven, which is our ultimate goal. Scripture makes it clear, that our hardships train us towards the ultimate qualities of godliness and love (2 Pet. 1:5-7). This is where we need to be. While our struggles may not lead to a reward in this world, they prepare us for things to come in the next life. Catholics believe these sufferings help purge our sins and develop characteristics now which we won't have to go through in purgatory. In other words, they help us get to the place where we need to be. The purification needed to make our souls ready for heaven will happen in this life or after death. Thus, troubles in this life will help us to obtain the perfection for which God is molding us that much sooner. For those who don't believe in purgatory, we must be content to trust in God's everlasting purposes that He knows what He is doing, and that "in all things God works for the good of those who love him, who have been called according to his purpose" (Romans 8:28 NIV).

THY ROD AND THY STAFF, THEY COMFORT ME

In his book, "A Shepherd Looks at Psalm 23," W. Phillip Keller describes how ancient shepherds in the Middle East and Africa used both rod and staff. The rod was essentially a weapon of defense and discipline. The rod could be propelled like a spear to hit a sheep who insisted on wandering away from the flock or towards danger. It could also be used as a club to kill snakes or fight off wild dogs that threatened the flock.

In His spiritual flock, our Lord uses his rod in much the same way. When we begin to wander away, the Holy Spirit may need to knock us on the head with a blow to make us realize that we are headed towards danger. Just as parents use discipline to instill right behavior and attitudes in their children that will serve them well as they grow, so God disciplines us, not out of anger or wrath, but to help us stay the course and learn right from wrong. "For the LORD disciplines him who He loves" (Heb 12:6 RSV). Pastor Bill Goddard used to preach that the opposite of love was not hate, but not caring. A good parent is one who loves her child and teaches the child right from wrong through the judicious use of discipline. A bad parent is one who doesn't care and never bothers to discipline the child. Scripture says, "Whoever spares the rod hates their children, but the one who loves their children is careful to discipline them" Prov 13:24 NIV). Someone observing a shepherd propel his rod against a stray sheep may accuse him of abuse, but the shepherd does so to prevent the death of the wandering lamb. It is well known that clear consistently enforced limits help children feel more secure and happy. So it is with us. When we realize that there is a God in heaven who cares for us, sets limits, and enforces them, we can feel a certain comfort in that fact.

Shepherds used their rods to fight wild beasts. David fought the lion and the bear to protect his flocks. Shepherds elsewhere may fight wild dogs, coyotes, wolves and snakes. Jesus said of Himself that He was the Good Shepherd laying His life down for the sheep. While He accepted the cross passively, He is no wimp. We look to Him for strength and help to fight off all types of evil and dangers in our lives on a daily basis. He is our fortress and our strong tower! This is why I commissioned from my artist friend, Rob Marshall, the cartoon illustrating this chapter-- Jesus as a Kung Fu fighter. We can see Him using His rod and staff to ward off all enemies to protect us, His sheep!

As many have pointed out over the centuries, the staff is the symbol of authority. Bishops in Catholic and Orthodox churches are given a staff to represent their authority over the Christians in their diocese. Jesus is the Great Shepherd over His entire worldwide church and the staff represents His authority. The staff, like the rod can be used to direct the sheep. Rather than using it for punishment, like the rod, or to inflict a blow to catch the sheep's attention, the hook of the staff may be used to gently put a lamb this way or that, or to touch the lamb to let him know of the shepherd's presence. Finally, the hook may also be used to lift a wayward lamb that has fallen into a crevice. The staff is the extension of the shepherd's hands to touch, to lift, to direct.

Our LORD touches us gently from time to time just to let us know He is there. This may be in a beautiful sunrise, the presence of a dove at an opportune time, or little signs and signals that we take to be signs from God. Perhaps it is a precious presence we feel during our prayers, that we know indeed that our God is with us. Maybe it is those goose pimples we feel while singing a beloved hymn or a phone call at just the right time. So many times our LORD reaches out to us, this way or that, to let us know He is here!

The staff may also be used as a hook to lift up and rescue lambs who have fallen down a crevice or who are stuck in a tight place. How many times have we fallen into a crevice of life, stumbling after some dumb decision we have made? Calling out in prayer, we cry, "LORD, help me!" God faithfully comes through, using His staff to snatch us up from danger. With His staff, the LORD restores our life to us. Thank you, LORD.

HIS HOLY COMFORT

David declared to the LORD in Psalm 23 that "Thy rod and thy staff, they comfort me" (Ps 23:4 KJV). Yes, God provides us comfort through His presence. David was comforted knowing that there was a God in heaven who loved Him and cared about Him. He was comforted in the knowledge that God cared enough to provide Him direction and would discipline Him if he got off track. He received comfort from the knowledge that God would protect him from his enemies and reach down and rescue him if his life was in danger. Finally, he found comfort in the occasional beauty surrounding him that assured him that God was present.

Not only did David experience this comfort from God, but so can we. Paul wrote, "Praise be to the God and Father of our LORD Jesus Christ, the Father of compassion and the God of all comfort, who comforts us in all of our troubles, so that we can comfort those in any trouble with the comfort we ourselves receive from God" (2 Cor 1:3-4 NIV). In other words, God continues to comfort and care for us, but now we need to take that encouragement, comfort, and love and pass it on to those around us. We need to pass it on!

There is much pain, heartache, sadness, and death in this world. Jesus experienced this pain personally in order to deliver us from its permanent effects. He conquered sin and death in the heavenly realms, but we still feel its temporary effect in our daily lives. He is here with us through these troubles, comforting us, lifting us, loving us. We should not just suck all this attention in forever, continuing to make Him nurse our wounds. We are also expected, through this pain, to grow and develop patience, perseverance, courage, and faith. Receiving God's comfort, and having survived the hard times, we can now turn to our brothers and sisters who continue to feel the pain and offer them the same hope and encouragement that we ourselves have received!

QUESTIONS

1. Give an example in your life where you needed to walk through the valley to reach the plateau.

2. Have you ever felt abandoned by God, only to discover later on that He was at work in those adverse circumstances?

3. How might your personal sufferings be "offered up" for the good of the body?

4. What are some ways that God has disciplined you in your lifetime? How did this discipline help you grow?

5. How does God let you know He is present in your daily life?

YOU PREPARE A TABLE: ©Ann Ostini

6.

A GOD WHO CELEBRATES

"Thou preparest a table before me in the presence of mine enemies" (Ps 23:5 KJV)

This has always been the most difficult verse of Psalm 23 for me to understand. Part of the problem is that David changes metaphors in the middle of his Psalm. For the last four verses we have been the sheep of the Good Shepherd, eating grass, drinking from still waters, and being protected from wolves and beasts by the strong arm of our Savior. But now, David switches gears. Just as in a dream, we are acting out one scenario in our minds, then suddenly we are somewhere else, so it is with the 23rd Psalm. Previously, we were sheep in the LORD's pasture; now suddenly, we are humans again sitting at the LORD's Table. We are His honored guests and He is our heavenly host.

This is the strange, yet wonderful, aspect of our Christian faith. While on one hand, He is the Almighty God, while we are His creatures who owe Him our obedience and love, fear and respect; on the other hand, He is our loving Father, our Gentle Shepherd, our Friend, and now our Heavenly Host. The same God whom the kings of the earth bow before in heaven and throw their crowns at His feet is the same God who became flesh and knelt down before His disciples with towel in hand to wash their feet. He is the same God who endured the suffering of the cross, to save us from our sins, and who eagerly desires us to call Him "Father" so that He can call us "My child." It is this God, whom David addresses as "You." This God, who as Shepherd loved us, fed us, led us, restored our lives to us, and protected us from evil, now as Host, rewards us with a feast!

Michael L. Faber

REWARD FOR A JOB WELL DONE

Even as protected sheep, with our Great Shepherd beside us, our lives have been arduous, and tiring. We have been on a great journey. We have walked many miles in valleys and mountains, through dry places and green. We have been in danger and we have been rescued. We have been obedient and we have wandered. We have been lost and then we have been found.

Our lives have definitely been mirrored in the metaphor of the sheep and the Shepherd which took place in the first four verses of this Psalm. As Christians, even though Christ is on our side, it has not always been easy for us to follow Him. Sometimes, we have had to endure financial and physical hardship, and we have been able to trust Him in varying degrees. Sometimes, sin has lured us away from the path, and Christ has had to throw His rod at us to get our attention or to gently pull us back with His staff. No matter where we have wandered, "If we confess our sins, He is faithful and just, and will forgive our sins" (1 John 1:9 RSV). We have been through foggy times when the leading of our God has not been all too clear, but we faithfully muddled through anyway, and He has made a way. We have been threatened by the forces of evil and danger and Christ has used His rod and staff to protect us.

While our lives as Christians are often hard, if we persevere, if we are faithful, there comes a time for God's reward. Paul speaks of this to the Corinthians: "Do you not know that in a race all the runners run, but only one gets the prize? Run in such a way as to get the prize. Everyone who competes in the games goes into strict training. They do it to get a crown that will not last, but we do it to get a crown that will last forever" (1 Cor 9:24-25 NIV). Praise the LORD, our race of life is not limited to only one winner. If we persevere to the end, we all have a chance to win, but we must be disciplined and "not run like someone running aimlessly" (1 Cor 9:26 NIV). Instead, "let us throw off everything that hinders and sin that so easily entangles. And let us run with perseverance the race marked out for us" (Heb 12:1). When we place our trust in Christ, and run our race and struggle against sin, we can be assured that we will suffer just like Jesus, but we must take heart from His example, "fixing our eyes on Jesus, the pioneer and perfecter of our faith. For the joy set before him he endured the cross, scorning its shame, and sat down at the right hand of the throne of God" (Heb 12:2 NIV). Jesus had a hard time in this life, but He had a clear picture of the joy that awaited Him in heaven, so He was strengthened to persist on His course. Likewise, we may suffer physical illness. We may suffer emotional and financial setbacks. We may even suffer persecution from evil people who oppose the gospel, but we must remember there is a reward waiting for us, if we endure to the end.

NOW AND LATER

In the 23rd Psalm, we were sheep in the field as we struggled through the vagaries of this life, but now is time for the reward.

What is this reward? Like all things spiritual, some of it begins now, and more of it awaits us in heaven! St. Augustine saw the table as a reward for spiritual maturity to be enjoyed in this life. He wrote, "The time for the rod has passed, that time when I was small and animal-like and was instructed amid the flocks in the pasture; now after that era of the rod I have begun to be guided under your staff, and now you have prepared a table before me, so that I may be no longer fed on milk like a baby, but as an adult eat solid food and be strengthened against those who oppress me" (Expositions on the Psalms 23.5). Others see it as the final reward in heaven.

David simply states, "You prepare a table before me" (Ps 23:5 NIV). It is a great table of feasting in the presence of the LORD. Before there was want, now there is plenty. Before there was fear, now there is comfort. Before there was darkness, now there is light. Before there was loneliness, and now there is the everlasting presence of the Father who has made us His guests and honors us for joining Him! We can look forward to the heavenly banquet. What is this heavenly banquet? We can read about it in Revelation 19. There, the apostle John has been swept up into heaven in a wonderful vision and he records the following scene,

"Then I heard what sounded like a great multitude, like the roar of rushing waters and like loud peals of thunder shouting: "Hallelujah! For our LORD God Almighty reigns. Let us rejoice and be glad and give him glory! For the wedding of the Lamb has come, and his bride has made herself ready. Fine linen, bright and clean, was given her to wear." (Fine linen stands for the righteous acts of God's holy people.) Then the angel said to me, "Write this: Blessed are those who are invited to the wedding supper of the Lamb!" And he added, "These are the true words of God." (Rev 19:6-10 NIV).

There is a great celebration going on in heaven, where the marriage of Christ and His Church is being celebrated for eternity. It is the Wedding Supper of the Lamb. We are invited to make ourselves ready. This feast is our reward for trusting and obeying Christ through thick and thin. It is our prize for running the race with discipline. It is the joy set before us in times of persecution. God is preparing our place at the table, even as you now read these words!

While these comments are geared towards our final heavenly reward, I agree with Augustine that there is a place at the table now as well. Not only is it the spiritual reward of maturity, and feasting on the meat of God's word as opposed to just the milk, as Augustine suggested, but it is also the table (the holy altar) set before us in Church.

When Jesus sat at the Passover table with His apostles, He took the bread and said, "This is my body given for you; do this in remembrance of me" (Luke 22:19 NIV). Then He took the cup and said, "This cup is the new covenant in my blood, which is poured out for you" (Luke 22:20 NIV). "Do this, whenever you drink it, in remembrance of me. (1 Cor 11:25 NIV). Paul asked the Corinthians, "Is not the cup of thanksgiving [Eucharist] for which we give thanks a participation in the blood of Christ? And is not the bread that we break a participation in the body of Christ?" (1 Cor. 10:16 NIV). As believers, we are invited to the table of Christ, to participate in His blood and in His body. He becomes our spiritual food and when we eat of the bread and drink of the cup, we receive Him, body, blood, soul, and divinity. Jesus states, "Very truly I tell you, unless you eat the flesh of the Son of Man and drink his blood, you have no life in you. Whoever eats my flesh and drinks my blood has eternal life, and I will raise him up at the last day. For my flesh is real food and my blood is real drink. Whoever eats my flesh and drinks my blood remains in me, and I in them" (John 6:53-56 NIV).

As New Covenant believers, not only do we have the hope of looking forward to the Celestial Marriage Supper of the Lamb in heaven as a final reward for our struggles and faithfulness on earth, but we may participate in the LORD's Supper here on earth. Christ, Himself becomes actually present in the elements of the table and invites us to receive Him and to nourish ourselves on His body, blood, soul, and divinity so that He can be in us and we can be in Him. This is the true essence of Communion! We are given the gift of Communion with Christ, "so the one who feeds on me will live because of me" (John 6:57 NIV).

So our table feast is already and not yet, like so many promises in Scripture. Already, we can join the heavenly feast of Revelation 19 as Christ offers Himself in the one-time eternal sacrifice. We can already feast on divine food and drink to nourish our soul. But we are not yet able to understand and experience this reward, and supernatural joy that awaits us, when we finally see our Heavenly Host as He is, face to face.

That's fine, you say, but what is this about my enemies?

IN THE PRESENCE OF MY ENEMIES

One of the jarring things about the psalms, including Psalm 23, is David's constant references to enemies. He will be going along with beautiful lofty language praising God, drawing our spirits into the heavenly realms, but then he seems to spoil the moment by returning to some reference to his enemies. Why all these references to enemies? Aren't we supposed to love everyone? If we love everyone as Christ commanded, how can we have any enemies? Aren't the existence of enemies an indication of the fact that we are not living as we should? Doesn't Paul admonish us, "If it is possible, as far as it depends on you, live at peace with everyone" (Romans 12:18 NIV)? Unfortunately, just as we will always have the poor among us, it is probable that we will also always have enemies. Even Jesus had enemies and He lived a sinless life. The writer of the Hebrews declares, "Consider Him who endured such opposition from sinners, so that you will not grow weary and lose heart" (Heb 12:3 NIV). Jesus is our example to keep going, even in the face of opposition. Living for God tends to arouse the hatred and jealousy of those who have decided to reject God. "In fact, everyone who wants to live a godly life in Christ Jesus will be persecuted" (2 Tim 3:12 NIV). Jesus Himself stated, "If the world hates you, keep in mind that it hated me first. If you belonged to the world, it would love you as its own. As it is, you do not belong to the world, but I have chosen you out of the world. That is why the world hates you" (John 15:18 NIV). This said, if you find you don't have any enemies, then perhaps you are doing something wrong! Perhaps you are compromising too much and remaining silent too much. Sinning like the rest of the world too much. Maintaining the attitudes of the flesh rather than the spirit too much. If so, the world will not reject you or hate you because you belong to the world.

Why do the righteous accrue enemies? One reason is spiritual, the other is psychological. On the spiritual side, Satan opposes the work of God and will do everything in his power to oppose and destroy the people of God. On the psychological side, those who choose to reject God and embrace sin feel a certain level of condemnation. The presence of those choosing righteousness makes them remember their guilt, even if the righteous say nothing directly to them about their sin. Paul mentions this concept when he writes, "For we are an aroma of Christ to God among those who are being saved and among those who are perishing, to one a fragrance from death to death, to the other a fragrance from life to life" (2 Cor 2:15-16 RSV). To those who are perishing, we remind them of their choice to deny life through Christ and their opposition to us is almost visceral.

When I was in boot camp, I once started a fight just by sleeping in the bathroom! I talked a lot about God to my buddies, which caused some to like me and some to hate me. It was not uncommon to be really tired during boot camp due to long hours and night watches. Sometimes any quiet time let straight to sleep. We did not have stalls on our toilets, and once I sat down and relaxed for a second, I found myself catching some zzzz's. One of the other soldiers saw me and announced loudly that I was "praying on the toilet." This announcement was peppered with profanities and immediately started an argument in the other room (which woke me up), about whether or not it was okay to pray in the bathroom! Point being, my presence (whether awake or asleep) caused these men to take sides. When people identify you as a Christian, they may change their language around you or even think of God and the claims of Christ when you enter the room. These thoughts will bring forth many reactions depending on whether they think of themselves as enemies or friends of God. If you are walking strongly in the faith, the enemies of God will hate you even before you meet them.

We have no idea if our enemies will be present in the afterlife. There is the story of the rich man and Lazarus where after death both the rich man and Lazarus were aware of each other's presence, even though a great chasm separated them. But this story could simply be a parable, rather than a description of the afterlife, or a description of Sheol prior to Christ's opening of heaven. It is unlikely that those in heaven will be aware of the suffering of those in hell, or the joys of heaven would be certainly diminished; although it is possible that those in hell will be aware of what they rejected, which would make their suffering worse. We simply don't know.

In this life, however, we can certainly experience David's imagery of being "in the presence of my enemies." While we may endure persecution from time to time, in this life, often we also may enjoy the temporal rewards of our good choices. While not always, sometimes, honesty, hard work, and a sober lifestyle lead to worldly success, a happy family, and a sense of joy and inner peace. Those around us who have opposed us because of their choice follow sin rather than faith may find themselves reaping the temporal rewards of sin such as a broken family, a destroyed career, imprisonment, alcoholism, addiction, or depression. Perhaps remembering an early time in life when they seemed to be on top with all the cool kids and hassled the nerds who refused to participate in their disobedient activities, they now find themselves on the bottom of society and envying the apparent success of those who made wise choices. This is a very common example of God laying out a table for His faithful in the presence of their enemies. Those on the outside may often envy the fruit of righteousness obtained by the faithful. Unfortunately, this may also make them redouble their opposition.

We can be certain that whatever the vagaries of this life's fortunes, whether we are rewarded by God or temporarily punished by our enemies for remaining faithful to the LORD, eventually all things will be made right and we will certainly enjoy that celestial table. Those who opposed us may be present in one way or another and able to see what they have missed out on.

QUESTIONS

1. How does the voice of Psalm 23 change in this verse?
2. How do you imagine heaven to be?
3. How is the Mass a foretaste of heaven?
4. Is it possible for a faithful Christian to avoid having enemies?
5. How should we behave towards our enemies?

7.

A GOD WHO ANOINTS

"Thou anointest my head with oil" (Ps 23:5 KJV)

As we are seated at the LORD's banquet, it is interesting to note that no food is mentioned. Rather, David speaks of oil and drink. This is not to say there is no food. Every banquet has food and earlier we saw the possibility that this food might be the LORD Himself, in the holy bread of Eucharist. But in this passage, the psalmist focuses on the anointing oil and the cup.

Michael L. Faber

WHAT IS THE OIL?

What is this oil which the psalmist speaks of? First of all, in the most literal sense, it was common for people in the dusty, dry air of the Ancient Near East to use oil for cosmetic purposes, smoothing it on their skin and their hair. In ancient Egypt, servants at a banquet or party would anoint the head of each guest as he took his seat. This may be the most basic image of the phrase. We have come to the LORD's table for our banquet and we are going to have our head anointed with oil. But wait! Notice it is not the servant who will do it. David says, "You anoint my head with oil" (Ps 23:5 NIV). In this picture, our Holy Host, our Great Shepherd, our everlasting God is doing the job reserved for servants. He is personally putting the oil on us for our comfort. This of course reminds us of the incident at the Last Supper when Jesus put a towel around His waist and proceeded to wash His disciple's feet. This was another job commonly left to servants prior to a meal. In performing this menial task, He reminded us that He had come to be the servant of all. So our God Himself serves us by putting oil on our heads for comfort. Perhaps it is His way of saying, "Well done, good and faithful servant! You have been faithful with a few things; I will put you in charge of many things. Come and share your master's happiness!" (Matt 25:23 NIV).

This is the most literal meaning. Of course, the oil can symbolize other more spiritual things as well. The oil also has a symbolic meaning in the Old and New Testaments.

In the Old Testament, the anointing with oil was a symbol of endowment with the Spirit of God for the duties of the office to which a person was consecrated. Moses anointed the altar,

Aaron, and Aaron's sons to consecrate them for service to God through the priesthood (Lev. 8:10-12). Samuel anointed Saul for the kingship over Israel by pouring a flask of oil on his head (1 Sam 10:1) and promising the Spirit would come on him to change him into a different person and empower him for the task ahead (1 Sam 10:6). Likewise, Samuel anointed David for his reign by pouring a flask of oil over his head, and "from that day on the Spirit of the LORD came powerfully upon David" (I Sam. 16:13, 14 NIV). The prophet Isaiah proclaimed in famous words, repeated by Christ, "The Spirit of the Sovereign LORD is on me, because the LORD has anointed me to proclaim good news to the poor" (Isa 61:1 NIV).

In the New Testament, we are not shown a physical anointing with oil for consecration, but the idea of being anointed with oil and the power of the Holy Spirit is continued in indirect remarks. Christ repeated the words of Isa 61:1, saying he was anointed to proclaim good news to the poor. (Luke 4:18 NIV). We hear Peter speak of Jesus saying "how God anointed Jesus of Nazareth with the Holy Spirit and power, and how he went around doing good and healing all who were under the power of the devil" (Acts 10:38 NIV).

There is a time in our sacramental life, as Catholics and/or Eastern Orthodox, that we are anointed with oil. The catechism teaches us, "From that time on [referring to Pentecost] the apostles, in fulfillment of Christ's will, imparted to the newly baptized by the laying on of hands the gift of the Spirit that completes the grace of Baptism" (CCC 1288). "Very early, the better to signify the gift of the Holy Spirit, an anointing with perfumed oil (chrism) was added to the laying on of hands. This anointing highlights the name 'Christian,' which means 'anointed' and derives from that of Christ himself whom God 'anointed with the Holy Spirit'" (CCC 1289). This sacrament is called confirmation in the West and chrismation in the East.

Thus, the link from Old Testament times, to New Testament, to modern is that anointing with oil is a powerful symbol of receipt of the gifts and the Gift of the Holy Spirit. This act completes the grace of baptism and is a great spiritual reward.

When we enter the sacramental life as a new Christian whether as baby or adult, we are entering the already/not yet condition of salvation. Salvation is the ultimate reward after a job well done. It is the final banquet table described by David in this Psalm, but it is also the state of being that Christians find themselves while still in this life. We are already saved, already written in the Lamb's Book of Life, already baptized, already confirmed, already filled with the Spirit, already enjoying some of the fruit of our salvation, some of the food from the table, some of the oil on our heads, yet Scripture also makes it clear that we are ***being saved*** through a process that is continuing and which we can choose to terminate. We are working out our salvation with fear and trembling (Phil 2:12). And we will be saved, when we are brought before the Great Throne of Judgment, the books are opened, and our eternal reward is pronounced.

WHAT IS THE CUP?

Imagine after a very hard and dangerous journey, you finally arrive at your destination. During the journey, you suffered privation and hardship. Many nights you were hungry or missed out on luxuries you have come to expect. Finally, upon arrival, you are greeted warmly by the host. He hugs you, takes your coat, and shows you to your seat. You have arrived just in time for the feast! As discussed above, he takes the role of a servant and puts perfumed oil on your head, so that you can relax. Spread out before you is every kind of food. As he pours you a drink, there is no indication of rationing like you had to do with your water when you were on the trail. There is no hint of selfishness or holding back. Rather, laughingly, he pours your drink, allowing it to run over the top. You know that when you are finished, there is more where that came from! This is the image that the psalmist paints for us in this verse. The time of hardship is over. The time of rejoicing and feasting has come! The LORD is our lavish host.

"You anoint my head with oil; my cup overflows" (Ps 23:5 NIV).

"What is the cup?" The cup is a sign of the extravagant love our God holds for us. We have spent our whole life as wandering sheep, and He has done everything in His power to guide us, lead us, protect us, and call us home when we have gone astray. Through His Son, Jesus Christ, He has even laid His life down for us to pay the price for our sins so that we could be reconciled to Him. As He hung on the cross, Jesus cried out, "I thirst." No doubt, He was physically thirsty and desired moisture for His parched lips. No doubt, he longed for the cup of thanksgiving, which He had drunk a few hours earlier with His beloved disciples, when He declared, "This cup is the new covenant in my blood, which is poured out for you" (Luke 22:20 NIV). But He was thirsty for something more than just liquid. He was thirsty for everlasting fellowship with the wandering souls who He had come to save. He was thirsty for fellowship with you and me. It was for us and for our friendship He came to die. We have spent our lifetimes wandering and looking away from Him. We have followed the lusts and passions of this world rather than our Savior, but the Good Shepherd has faithfully and longingly called us back. By the power of His grace, He has succeeded. We crossed the finish line! We have come home to His heavenly glory. We have turned to His loving embrace, sat at His bountiful table, and now we have His cup before us. This is the cup of the new and everlasting covenant which He so graciously, so generously, and so extravagantly poured for us, to the point of overflowing! Drink from it, and there will be more. It is the cup of God's most bountiful love.

THE CUP OF THE MOST EXCELLENT INEBRIATION

An interesting side note on the cup. By the time of Christ and during the early Church, the Hebrew Old Testament had fallen out of use and the Greek translation of the Old Testament, (commonly referred to as the LXX), was more commonly used. Scholars have found that sometimes there are slight variations of wording between certain Old Testament passages in the Greek and in the Hebrew. Modern English translations typically translate from the Hebrew Scripture rather than the Greek. Therefore, sometimes the words in Scripture quoted by New Testament writers and early church fathers vary somewhat from what we are used to hearing. Psalm 23:5 is one of those places where there is a variance. In the Greek version it says something to the effect of "your cup inebriates most excellently." The English translation by Sir Lancelot C.L Brenton, tames this somewhat by saying, "thy cup cheers me like the best wine." As discussed above, the Hebrew from which our modern English Bibles come from says "my cup runneth over" or "my cup overflows." The difference between your cup and my cup is moot. We are the guests sitting at the LORD's banquet. He has set the silverware which all belongs to Him whether or not we are using it. The interesting difference I noted was that in the Greek version, it is explicitly stated that the guest is intoxicated presumably with the best wine, while this is only implied in the Hebrew. The Greek phrase brings to mind the story of Jesus at the Wedding in Cana. The host had run out of wine, and with the intervention of Mary, Jesus was persuaded to save the day. He turned the water to wine. When they tasted it, the guests were surprised that the host had saved the most excellent wine for last. Whatever God does is always the most excellent. Since the early church used the Greek version of the old testament, the early church commentators spoke of this cup of inebriation.

In general, both the Old Testament and the New Testament condemn drunkenness. "Wine is a mocker and beer a brawler; whoever is led astray by them is not wise" (Prov. 20:1 NIV), "Do not get drunk on wine, which leads to debauchery. Instead, be filled with the Spirit" (Eph 5:18 NIV). But the early church fathers saw this intoxication at the LORD's table as a good kind, not the bad kind. A sixth century bishop, Fulgentius of Ruspe, opined that the drunkenness which one received from the LORD's cup "poured into the inner depths of the heart so that every affection of the heart, overcome is assigned to oblivion." In other words, the cup helped us to abandon the things of the world that are contrary to the love of Christ and to focus on him more fully. Theophilus of Alexandria saw the cup of inebriation as one that provided exultation of immortality and wine that eased the pains of the wounds we have suffered in this life. Bishop Ambrose, the mentor of St. Augustine, saw the cup that inebriates as a powerful tonic to wash away every stain of sin. I like to think of it as simply a cup of everlasting joy. For those that have experienced intoxication there is a great deal of joy and mirth in that state. Unfortunately, later, one pays the price with the hangover, the possibility of alcoholism, and all the pain which ensues from that condition. This cup, however, gives us joy and a sense of wellness that comes with no ill after effects, because it is from the LORD. Notice that the text only refers to the cup of the most excellent inebriation, it does not say this inebriation comes from alcohol. I like to think it comes straight from the Holy Spirit. Paul says, "Do not be drunk on wine…Instead be filled with the Spirit" (Eph 5:18 NIV). While he doesn't say it explicitly, the Spirit brings its own exultation, joy, and sometimes even silliness, but it is the good kind of inebriation that brings only the joy without the ensuing debauchery or hangover.

Scripture declares that joy is a fruit of the Spirit (Gal 5:22). As a fruit, it should grow naturally in everyone who abides in the Spirit. It is not a gift, given only to some as the Spirit wills, but a fruit which comes to all. Heaven will be a place of great joy, a place of the most excellent inebriation. I imagine in heaven, there will be nothing but pure joy. Once, when I was in my early thirties, a group of my friends and I were meeting regularly on Friday nights to worship and praise the LORD. We would regularly meet for three or four hours at a time. We made it a habit during these sessions to divide up into separate rooms and pray for 15 or 20 minutes and then to come back and share with each other our experiences. One of these nights, I began laughing in my room, for no apparent reason. After that, this feeling of joy poured over me and into me. It was so intense I though my head was going to explode. I was biting down on the chain of my cross necklace. Then a voice said to me in my thoughts, "If you saw My face, you would die. Your body is not equipped to handle the full joy you will experience in heaven, this is just a foretaste!" That was it. Then the experience was over. The most interesting thing I discovered, after I went back into the living room to report my experience, was that the others had not heard a voice or experienced the joy, but each of them said that for some reason, in their separate rooms, they had also started laughing! This had never happened to us before and never happened again. Later, someone suggested to us that this was the Toronto blessing, but we had never heard of such a thing. The point of this story is, that heaven is a place of great joy-joy beyond our imagination.

"But as it is written, Eye hath not seen, nor ear heard, neither have entered into the heart of man, the things which God hath prepared for them that love him" (1 Cor 2:9 KJV). You don't need to believe my vision, but the words of Scripture are clear: great joy awaits us in heaven.

QUESTIONS

1. How do you understand the idea already saved, but not yet?

2. What kind of gifts did you get at your confirmation? Why do so many confirmed Christians seem to lack these gifts in their daily life?

3. Have you ever felt "drunk in the Spirit" or had an intense supernatural joy come over you during worship?

4. What does it mean that joy is a fruit of the spirit and not a gift of the spirit?

5. Do you have joy in your walk with Christ? If not, why not? What could you do to change this?

8.

A GOD WHOSE MERCY IS BEFORE AND AFTER

"Surely goodness and mercy shall follow me all the days of my life" (Ps 23:6 KJV)

As people of God's pasture, goodness is our goal, and mercy is our gift. Often words like goodness and mercy don't mean much to us if we don't think about them. This line flows from our lips like a fitting musical ending to a beautiful psalm. We should try to meditate even on these last words, lest we become like little Timmy in a joke I saw on the internet! It goes as follows:

> Timmy was a little five-year-old boy that his Mom loved very much and being a worrier, she was concerned about him walking to school when he started Kindergarten. She walked him to school the first couple of days, but when he came home one day, he told his mother that he did not

want her walking him to school every day. He wanted to be like the big boys.

He protested loudly, so she had an idea of how to handle it. She asked a neighbor, Mrs. Goodnest, if she would surreptitiously follow her son to school, at a distance behind him that he would not likely notice, but close enough to keep a watch on him. Mrs. Goodnest said that since she was up early with her toddler anyway, it would be a good way for them to get some exercise as well so she agreed.

The next school day, Mrs. Goodnest and her little girl, Marcy, set out following behind Timmy as he walked to school with another neighbor boy he knew. She did this for the whole week. As the boys walked and chatted, kicking stones and twigs, the little friend of Timmy noticed that this same lady was following them as she seemed to do every day all week.

Finally, he said to Timmy, "Have you noticed that lady following us all week? Do you know her?"

Timmy nonchalantly replied, "Yea, I know who she is."

The little friend said, "Well who is she?" "That's just Shirley Goodnest," Timmy said. "Shirley Goodnest? Who the heck is she and why is she following us?"

"Well," Timmy explained, "every night my Mom makes me say the 23rd Psalm with my prayers 'cuz she worries about me so much. And in it, the prayer psalm says, "Shirley Goodnest and Marcy shall follow me all the days of my life. So I guess I'll just have to get used to it." (Dave

Palmer, "Goodness and Mercy," www.theblackriver.net/attic/shirleygoodnest.html)

GOODNESS AND MERCY AS OUR GIFT TO OTHERS

These words, "Surely goodness and mercy shall follow me all the days of my life" (Ps 23:6 KJV) are a wonderful sentiment taken from the last verse of our most beloved Psalm 23. In the past, I always used to interpret these words as something to the effect of "If I am a child of God, God's goodness and mercy will be with me through the rest of my life." It was like the expression of a promise or a hope. Certainly, that is a true statement. We have already seen how when the LORD is our shepherd, He sustains us, guides us, communicates with us, protects us, restores our spirit, and rewards us with His everlasting banquet and His most excellent cup of joy. If these words, mean as I thought, that goodness and mercy will be with me for the rest of my life, then they are just a recapitulation or restatement of everything already said.

But, what if they mean something else? Notice in this statement the tiny word "follow." Goodness and Mercy aren't said to be with me, but they are said to follow me. To follow means to come after. Imagine a parade. First you have the little girl with the baton at the beginning of the parade, and following after her are the horses, the cars, the marching bands, and the floats. When you see the little girl with the baton, you have an expectation based on your experience of what will follow. As a Christian, you have certainly enjoyed God's goodness and mercy, as expressed in the entire Psalm, but if you are doing things right goodness and mercy should follow you as well! When my kids were smaller, if we went on a hike or to the park, I would always try to tell them, "Let's leave the park or the trail cleaner than we found it." I would then encourage them not only to avoid littering, but also to pick up someone else's litter as well. At the end of the hike or the excursion we would throw away the garbage we found and feel good about leaving behind a cleaner place than we found it.

This is exactly what we should be doing in our daily lives as Christians. When we wake up and interact with the world, we need to first avoid littering. We should do our best to avoid sinning against others, hurting feelings, wounding souls, and acting with selfishness or indifference. We need to avoid making the world worse off than we find it. For some of us, this is challenge enough. This is not our calling, however. We should also try to leave the world better than we found it. We need to be bearers of God's goodness and mercy to a hurting and dying generation. Are there lonely souls who need a word of encouragement? Are there beggars who need a dollar or two? Are there young people in need of a word of correction? Are there sick or lonely people, including parents or family, that could use a phone call or a visit? Is there a charity in need of a donation? Is there a grieving person in need of a hug? Is there someone without faith who needs to hear the gospel presented in a loving way? Remember, as a Christian, you are a member of the body of Christ, and as such, you represent Christ to the world? What would Jesus do in this situation?

As Paul put it, we are ambassadors for Christ. The world may not pick up a Bible and read it, but they know that you claim to be a Christian. Perhaps your life is the only Bible they will ever read. What will they learn about Jesus by watching you?

If you are doing what you should, everywhere you go, you will be reconciling people to God by your works as well as your words. In the gospel, Jesus commands us, "Be merciful just as your Father is merciful" (Luke 6:36 NIV). This type of mercy is not letting people off the hook when they do bad, but rather showing God's love and compassion to those who need it most. When you leave a place, you will leave God's goodness and mercy behind you? Goodness should be our goal but mercy our gift. Wherever we go, we should leave these things behind us.

GOD'S MERCY PRECEDES AND FOLLOWS US

I sat at the breakfast table across from my good friend Mike Davis. He recounted to me how he had a hard life. He was raised by a godly mother and grandmother and also guided by the discipline of his father who was often serving overseas. He was taught to love God and go to church and respect his parents. But once he got out of the house and out on his own, things began to go sideways. Alcohol abuse led to failed marriages and petty criminal offenses. According to him, all of his friends thought he was a "bad man." Even when he returned to church in his sixties's, his heart wasn't in it, until finally a DUI charge sent him to jail. During this time, he got involved in a Bible study with his fellow prisoners and was hit with the epiphany that alcohol was what put him there and undergirded all of his misery for the last 40 years. In that jail cell, he recommitted his life to Christ and has been growing stronger in his faith and staying away from alcohol ever since! That was almost ten years ago!

While the psalmist only speaks of mercy following us, a number of ancient commentators on this psalm meditated on how God's mercy both precedes us and follows us. Cassiodorus, a monk who lived in the AD 500s and who founded the Vivarium monastery in Calabria wrote, "Though the LORD's mercy always goes before us, he says here that it "will follow me". It follows particularly to protect, but it precedes to bestow grace. If it merely followed, no one would observe its gifts, and if it merely preceded, none could keep what is bestowed" (Cassiodorus, Explanation of the Psalms 23.6). Thus, God's goodness and mercy, in the words of Cassiodorus are guiding us to truth and are watching our backs!

Mike Davis experienced God's mercy preceding him when he was born into a Christian family who educated him and gave him a foundational knowledge of the truth. On his own, he departed that foundation and that truth and reaped the whirlwind in his personal life. Fortunately, God's mercy was also following behind him, dogging his every step until it could catch up to him in that jail cell. He now walks side by side with that mercy as it accompanies him in his now restored Christian life.

Without God's mercy following us all the days of our lives, we might be like the seeds that landed on shallow soil and sprung up but were quickly scorched by the sun. God's mercy preserves us in our initial good intentions. Speaking of mercy going before and after, St. Augustine adds these words, "Indeed we also work, but we are only collaborating with God who works, for his mercy has gone before us. It has gone before us that we may be healed, and follows us so that once healed we may be given life; it goes before us so that we may be called, and follows us so that we may be glorified; it goes before us so that we may live devoutly, and follows us so that we may always live with God: for without him we can do nothing" (St. Augustine, De natura et gratia, 31: PL 44, 264).

ALL THE DAYS OF MY LIFE

Once I was lamenting to a priest about how disappointed I was about the faith status and life choices of my son. I was truly grieved and fearful. I still am. The priest comforted me with these words. "It's not over until it's over. You don't know the end of the story. You are only looking at this point of time." He was right. If I were Mike Davis's dad looking at his life in his twenties I would have grieved, not knowing that it wouldn't be until his sixties that Mike turned around and got right with the Lord. Mike's dad didn't live to see those days.

Likewise, we don't know what the LORD will do with our loved ones or when he will do it. I take comfort that my son was baptized and confirmed in the Catholic Church. He has been adopted as a child of God, given the Spirit of God, marked, and had spiritual gifts poured into him by God. Now it is up to God's goodness and mercy to follow him all the days of his life until they catch up! I share these personal thoughts, because I know there are many parents and grandparents who are currently very worried about their children and grandchildren. At my men's group, which is comprised of men mostly 55+, the conversation frequently turns to our concern about our adult children who have "left the faith." Every now and then, we hear a praise testimony about one who has "returned to the fold."

God doesn't give up. He never gives up! It would be great if we could be baptized as children, stay chaste and pure as teenagers and young adults, and then live faithfully as mature and productive Christians for the rest of our lives. What a blessing. That happens sometimes, but more frequently, due to the distractions of this world, we see a great falling away among the young, with some but not all returning later in life.

I spent a great portion of my twenties away from the LORD, even though I was a fervent believer in high school. Statistics say that 2/3 of the youth active in church groups, both Protestant and Catholic, will fall away soon after they leave home. Eventually, the LORD used my uncle Vernon's funeral to begin calling me back. He was referred to as a "Man of God." I once considered myself that in high school, but now, years later, would anyone think that of me if I were to suddenly die? Like the old question goes, if someone were to accuse me of being a Christian, would there be enough evidence to convict? That started me thinking. Then several years later, the testimony of my friend really sealed my recommitment at age 30. He began coming around my house preaching to me that I needed to re-commit my life to Christ. I never considered myself lost to the faith, but I certainly wasn't living it. Now at age 30, I began faithfully attending church, studying the word of God and serving in ministry. God's mercy was following me all during the decade of my twenties. It never left me, but took ten years to catch up and really grab me.

St. Augustine was born to a pagan father and a Christian mother, St. Monica. In his young adult years, he practiced sexual immorality and explored various strange religions and cults. His mother constantly prayed that he would come to the Christian faith, but he held her beliefs in disdain as simplistic.

She prayed fervently for him for decades, until in his forties he happened to see a New Testament laying open in his garden and heard the voices of children chanting, "Pick up and read, pick up and read." He followed that leading and soon after converted, becoming one of the most famous and prolific theologians in Christian history! He was even appointed bishop of Hippo. His mother lived to see his conversion, but not his later success in the Church. For her, to know her beloved son had returned to Jesus was enough for her. God's mercy preceded and followed Augustine throughout his youth and young adulthood. This mercy was fueled by the prayers of his faithful mother, St. Monica. We too can pray for our wayward children, adding power to the Spirit's work. St. Monica's husband Patricius also converted on his death bed, no doubt due to the persistent prayers of his beloved wife, Monica. Catholics often ask St. Monica to join with them in prayers for their children. Below is an example of one such prayer:

> Dear St. Monica, troubled wife and mother,
> Many sorrows pierced your heart during your lifetime.
> Yet you never despaired or lost faith.
> With confidence, persistence and profound faith,
> you prayed daily for the conversion
> of your beloved husband, Patricius,
> and your beloved son, Augustine.
>
> Grant me that same fortitude, patience and trust in the Lord.
> Intercede for me, dear St. Monica, for *(mention your petition here)*
> and grant me the grace to accept his will in all things,
> through Jesus Christ, our Lord,

in the unity of the Holy Spirit,
one God forever and ever. Amen.

QUESTIONS

1. In your Christian walk, how have you brought goodness and mercy to others?

2. What kind of things could you begin doing to bring more goodness and mercy to people around you?

3. Were there any miracles or interesting events that led you to decide to live a faithful life for Jesus?

4. How has God showed you mercy to help you preserve your walk of faith?

5. What is the best way to bring a wayward child back to the faith?

9.

A GOD OF ETERNAL ABIDING

"and I will dwell in the house of the LORD for ever" (Ps 23:6 KJV).

In our modern mentality, dwelling in the LORD's house forever may or may not seem like a wonderful prospect. After all, wouldn't we rather have our own place rather than being a guest in someone else's place? It is great to be served as a guest, but you feel like you can't stretch out and be yourself, and you must act in your best behavior to avoid offending a host. Dwelling any place *forever* also has its problems. Isn't variety the spice of life? No matter where we live on earth, we tend to get tired of it and desire something else. If we live in a tropical environment, we wish for crisp alpine air and green pine trees. If we live in the mountains, we wish we could stay at the beach. Of course, if we assume that eternity has two destinations only, heaven and hell, we would much rather be a guest in the house of the LORD forever, than suffer the alternative!

This whole discussion is superficial and wrong, however, because we are looking at the psalmists words with worldly eyes and worldly attitudes that won't exist when we come to the presence of the Almighty God! If we are blessed to enter the house of the LORD, we simply won't want to be anywhere else and I don't believe we could even imagine being anywhere else. David attempts to describe the house of the LORD in Psalm 84 with these words:

> How lovely is your dwelling place,
> LORD Almighty!
> My soul yearns, even faints
> for the courts of the LORD;
> my heart and my flesh cry out
> for the Living God. (Ps 84:1-2 NIV).

What I am about to write may be offensive to some, but I believe it to be the truth. For some people, being in church or participating in worship or Bible study is wearisome toil. They look at the watch and make plans for what they can do after church is over. These people are not yet fit for heaven. For them, going to church is an obligation to please others, maintain a reputation, or perhaps a task to be done to avoid some type of earthly or heavenly punishment. For them, being in heaven might seem like a wearisome and toilsome fate if it meant worshiping God for all eternity. They have not yet learned to love the LORD. For others, they look forward to going to church. They love singing praises to the LORD. They enjoy reading the word of God and being around the people of God. These people are ready for heaven. Heaven is being in the presence of God forever. For those who truly love the LORD and His people, there could be no better place to exist.

David continues the psalm,

> Even the sparrow has found a home,
> and the swallow a nest for herself,
> where she may have her young—
> a place near Your altar.
> LORD Almighty, my King and my God.
> Blessed are those who dwell in your house;
> they are ever praising you.
> Blessed are those whose strength is in you
> Whose hearts are set on pilgrimage. (Ps 84:3-5 NIV).

For people bound to heaven, being near the LORD is a comfort. It is a source of blessing and strength. When we go to heaven and dwell in the house of the LORD, we will be ever praising God.

Remember the story I shared a few chapters back about the experience I had when the joy of the LORD descended upon me in that room? It was so intense; the blood veins were popping in my neck and I felt God tell me that if I experienced His full presence I would die. Believe me, for those seconds or few minutes, however long that experience lasted, I had no thoughts of wanting my own place, or needing to go somewhere else for a change. The immense level of joy, and pleasure of experiencing the presence of God was so overwhelming, I understood, why no one would be bored in heaven! To be **near** to God is everything.

David, continuing his psalm said,

> Better is one day in your courts
> Than a thousand elsewhere; (Ps 84:10 NIV).

I can understand this, if heaven is anything like what I experienced that Friday night in the room. The beach and the mountains cannot compare to the sheer joy and pleasure of being in the presence of the LORD. David says one day here is better than a thousand elsewhere, but we are not promised only one day. We are promised an *eternity*! "I will dwell in the house of the LORD forever!" (Ps 23:6 NIV).

Contemplating eternity is very difficult for the finite mind, but I think of the final verse in the hymn *Amazing Grace*.

> When we've been there ten thousand years
> Bright shining as the sun,
> We've no less days to sing Your praise
> Than when we'd first begun.

Yes, one day in God's presence is better than a thousand days elsewhere, but we have much more than just one day! Even after ten thousand years, we will still have just as much time in heaven as when we first got there because eternity is forever. It has no end.

HEAVEN VERSUS THE ALTERNATIVE

While heaven seems boring for some, they know they don't want to go to hell, so they grudgingly follow along with the Christian program of faith and worship. I can understand why. If anyone truly believed that hell exists, they would do everything they could to keep from going there. They would believe what needed to be believed and do what needed to be done. This is a sorry motivation for following the Christian faith. I wonder, when Judgment Day comes, if that will be enough.

Let me frame the proposition in another way. If anyone truly understood what heaven was, and truly believed that it existed, they would do anything they could to get there! People work hard, spend many years in school, and put up with a lot of personal grievance to climb the career ladder, because they know that it will give them a better chance for promotion and salary increase so that they can live a life of relative comfort and ease. Perhaps they want to travel, wear nice clothes, eat good food and not worry about bills. So they work and work and work so that they can have that pleasure for a few decades once they have reached the top, before they get old and get sick and die.

God gives us something far better than a few decades of comfort and wealth before sickness and death. He offers us the prospect of eternity in heaven, in His presence, where comfort and joy will last forever!

David knows this reward is far better than anything the career track can offer. He writes,

> I would rather be a doorkeeper in the house of my God
> than to dwell in the tents of the wicked.
> For the LORD God is a sun and shield;
> the LORD bestows favor and honor;
> no good thing does he withhold from those
> whose walk is blameless. (Ps 84:10-11 NIV).

A doorkeeper doesn't dwell inside the tent. He stands in the space between inside and outside. He is working and guarding, not laying around, eating and drinking and sleeping within the comfort of the tent. David declares that being a doorkeeper in the house of God is better than having full dwelling rights to the tents of the wicked. Why? It is not the house that counts, but who the house belongs to. Who dwells within that house means everything! Even standing at the door of the house of God, David nearer to God than he would be if he were dwelling with full rights in the tent of the wicked. Proximity to God is an indication of the level of joy one will have.

The closer we are to God, the more joyful our existence. Yes, perhaps we can attain a higher position, more wealth, and more power by following the ways of the wicked, but the rewards of wickedness are temporary and fleeting. The reward of the righteous is eternal. What is that reward? Being close to God. Proximity to God is an indication of the joy we will have not just now, but for all eternity. God is love. God is joy. Being close to Him is everything. Being far from Him or absent from Him is the definition of hell!

When we place our faith in Christ and enter into His family through baptism, we receive the Holy Spirit, the very spiritual DNA of God. As we grow and allow the Spirit to lead us, we learn to love our Father God more and more. The closer we grow to Him, the more we will follow His commands and the more we will love Him. By attending Mass, reading the Bible, participating in the sacraments, and repenting of sin, our love for Him grows, we obey Him more, and we enjoy our time with Him in greater measure. Unfortunately, the opposite is also true. If we ignore God and disobey His commands, we will feel alienation towards our Father in heaven. As sin grows in our hearts, we may even come to hate God, His word, and

His people. Jesus warned, "Therefore consider carefully how you listen. Whoever has will be given more; whoever does not have, even what they thinks they have will be taken from them" (Luke 8:18 NIV) If we leave our lives in a lukewarm condition, we will not desire heaven and God will honor our wishes. Our job here on earth, is to learn to follow God, trust Him and love Him. We are literally the sheep of His pasture and He is our Shepherd. Let us grow in faith and love towards our Good Shepherd, then we will learn to love Him and obey Him. As we grow in our love, heaven will seem like an increasingly wonderful place, and our desire will be only to spend all of eternity in the house of the LORD, just as David described. If we leave earth in this condition, heaven will be our chief desire. Our Father will honor that desire and bring us home to His heavenly house.

QUESTIONS

1. Does heaven seem boring to you? Why?

2. Do you truly look forward to attending Mass? Why? Why not?

3. What can we do to increase our love for the things of God?

4. What might happen to those who go along with the program to avoid hell, but don't really love the things of God?

5. How do you imagine heaven to be?

ABOUT THE AUTHOR

Michael Faber has published a number of books and articles about the Christian faith since 1993. He was originally given a license to preach by a small Baptist church in 1995, and then received a Master of Arts degree in theology and Bible from Fuller Seminary in 2012. As a Protestant, he served as interim pastor and guest preacher at several Baptist and Presbyterian churches. In 2016, he entered into full communion with the Roman Catholic Church and is now serving as coordinator of RCIA for his parish, as well as being active in the Catholic Cursillo movement. Mr. Faber has published the following books: *Meditations on the Lord's Prayer; Meditations on the Lord's Prayer Catholic Edition; Keys to a Happy Life: the Beatitudes According to Jesus, and Seven Word's of Jesus from the Cross.* Some of these books have been translated to Vietnamese and Telugu and distributed in Vietnam as well as India. He publishes weekly articles about faith and morals on his email blog. To subscribe free of charge and to receive these articles in your email, you may send your request to Mr. Faber at mfaber@elkgrove.net.

ACKNOWLEDGMENTS

I wish to thank Ann Ostini for the two beautiful paintings which illustrate this book. Thanks are due also to Rob Marshall, now Rob Rivera, who drew the exciting Kung Fu Jesus animation to illustrate the A God With Us chapter. Thank you to Julie Williams who faithfully helped me format my manuscript for publication and designed my book cover. Thanks to Jim Lehe for helping me with a suitable title for the book.

Great thanks are also given to a fellow Fuller Seminary graduate, Sara Lawson, who took a great deal of time to exhuastively edit the manuscript of this book. I didn't apply every single edit, so any remaining mistakes are probably mine.

This book never would have happened if it weren't for the beautiful people at Grace Presbyterian Church, and their pastor, Philip Trinh, who allowed me to preach most of the chapters in this book during my Psalm 23 preaching series. I preached the core of most of the earlier chapters of this book in 2015 and 2016. After preaching, I set to writing and interacted a little more methodically with the catechism and the Church Fathers after the fact. If I didn't preach the series, I probably never would have had the discipline to sit down and put out a book. Because I was in the process of coming into the Catholic Church at the time, my congregation probably heard a little more about the Catholic doctrine I was learning than they expected. I also thank them for gracefully and lovingly releasing me to the Catholic Church in the Spring of 2016.

Of course, my deepest thanks are to the Catholic Church which has preserved the thoughts and meditations of 2000 years of holy men and women, some of whose thoughts about Psalm 23, have been shared with you throughout the pages of this book.

www.ingramcontent.com/pod-product-compliance
Lightning Source LLC
Chambersburg PA
CBHW041318110526
44591CB00021B/2829